Julius Lloyd

Sermons on Old Testament characters

Julius Lloyd

Sermons on Old Testament characters

ISBN/EAN: 9783743305472

Manufactured in Europe, USA, Canada, Australia, Japa

Cover: Foto ©Lupo / pixelio.de

Manufactured and distributed by brebook publishing software (www.brebook.com)

Julius Lloyd

Sermons on Old Testament characters

SERMONS ON OLD TESTAMENT CHARACTERS

SERMONS

ON

OLD TESTAMENT CHARACTERS

BY THE

REV. JULIUS LLOYD, M.A.

HONORARY CANON OF MANCHESTER

AUTHOR OF "CHRISTIAN POLITICS," "THE NORTH
AFRICAN CHURCH," ETC.

LONDON

GEORGE BELL AND SONS, YORK STREET
COVENT GARDEN

1887

CHISWICK PRESS:—C. WHITTINGHAM AND CO., TOOKS COURT,
CHANCERY LANE.

PREFACE.

THE following Sermons are chiefly studies of life and character, drawn from the narrative portions of the Old Testament. They are intended to illustrate the moral use of Bible history, as Theology teaching by examples, in several stages of human progress. At the same time the typical significance of persons and incidents, which fills a large place in ecclesiastical literature, is not ignored. References are given to the Lectionary when, as in most cases, the subjects occur in the Sunday Lessons.

LEESFIELD VICARAGE, OLDHAM,
August, 1887.

CONTENTS.

		PAGE
1.	ADAM (Septuagesima) .	1
2.	NOAH (Sexagesima)	13
3.	ABRAHAM (Quinquagesima)	26
4.	ISAAC	38
5.	ESAU	50
6.	JACOB (Second Sunday in Lent) . .	63
7.	JOSEPH (Third Sunday in Lent) . .	75
8.	MOSES (Fifth Sunday in Lent) . . .	88
9.	KORAH (First Sunday after Easter) . .	99
10.	BALAAM (Third Sunday after Easter) . .	111
11.	JOSHUA (First Sunday after Trinity) .	123
12.	SAMSON	135
13.	BOAZ	146
14.	SAUL (Fourth Sunday after Trinity) .	157
15.	DAVID (Fifth Sunday after Trinity) . .	169
16.	RIZPAH	182
17.	KING DAVID (Seventh Sunday after Trinity).	194
18.	SOLOMON (Eighth Sunday after Trinity) .	205
19.	JEROBOAM (Tenth Sunday after Trinity) .	217
20.	AHAB (Eleventh Sunday after Trinity) . .	229

		PAGE
21.	ELIJAH (Eleventh Sunday after Trinity)	241
22.	MICAIAH (Twelfth Sunday after Trinity)	253
23.	NAAMAN (Thirteenth Sunday after Trinity)	265
24.	JEZEBEL (Fourteenth Sunday after Trinity)	277
25.	JOSIAH (Fifteenth Sunday after Trinity)	288
26.	ESTHER	301

SERMONS ON OLD TESTAMENT CHARACTERS.

I. ADAM.

"Of the tree of the knowledge of good and evil, thou shalt not eat." *Genesis*, ii. 17.

(𝔖eptuagesima, P.M.)

IT has been said of more than one famous picture that, if you look into the canvas closely, you see no distinct form; but if you survey the whole from a proper distance, the figures appear to be full of life. Something like this is the case when we read the description in Genesis of the primitive state of man, the Temptation and the Fall. The wisest expositors have been readiest to acknowledge a mystery beyond their understanding in the particulars of this description. Yet the story as a whole conveys a moral lesson, which is so plain as to make a deep impression on the minds of the youngest children, and at the same time so suggestive, that the eldest among us may study it profitably, as applicable to some of the deepest questions of human life.

Adam and Eve are described at the first as rational beings. Their task in the garden of Eden, to dress it and to keep it, implies an intelligent control over nature, which is one of the chief human prerogatives, being the first principle of all the arts. Moreover, in giving names to the animals Adam exercises a faculty of articulate speech, and of classification, in which the first principle of all the sciences is involved. Thus our first parents, in their state of innocence, are represented as endowed with those qualities which are the rudiments of skill and knowledge in every form.

But there is another kind of knowledge, the knowledge of good and evil, which God has forbidden to them, whether as a trial of obedience, or as a command like that of a wise parent, who restricts a young child's reading to books which are fit for his age. They are tempted by the serpent to seek that forbidden knowledge, and break the command. Eve sees that the fruit of the tree is good for food, and pleasant to the eyes, and she desires to be as God, knowing good and evil. So temptation comes in a three-fold form, through the appetite, the senses, and the mind. St. John's words, "the lust of the flesh, and the lust of the eyes, and the pride of life," denote the three forms of Eve's temptation, the three forms of the temptation of our Lord Jesus Christ, and the three forms in which temptation comes to every one of us. We see an example of the lust of the flesh in any drunkard or profligate; we see examples of the lust of the eyes in those who are given up to dress, jewelry, and the looking-glass; we see examples of the pride of life in self-complacent people of all kinds, who flatter themselves that they are as gods, knowing all they need to know.

Thus the Fall of our first parents is a true representation of human life in general. It sums up in its moral the fruits of experience ripened in many generations. I do not say for all, but for many, there is a bitter remembrance of having fallen from a state of innocence in a similar way, stretching out the hand to gratify the palate, or seeking to please the eye, or indulging the curiosity of the mind, and thereby losing the simple happiness of a good conscience at peace with God. The consequence of transgression in the character of Adam and Eve is true to life in every age. Their eyes were opened, and they were afraid of God's presence. Knowledge of good and evil brought to them the distressing self-consciousness, which is called a sense of shame. Hitherto they had no thought of concealment or covering, and the presence of God had been without terror to them; as we may see a little child daring to converse boldly with a great personage of whom his parents stand in awe.

Shame is a trouble of mind which affects the bodily frame, making the eyes look downward, and impelling the blood to the face. It is a sign, characteristic of human nature, of the conflict of good and evil in our souls, which proceeds from the knowledge of both. To be ashamed is not a proof of absolute sinfulness, nor of absolute holiness, but of a mixed state, in which the two extremes of sin and holiness contend together. Pure innocence feels no shame. Hardened guilt feels no shame. The sense of shame is acute in proportion to the consciousness of a discord between what we are and what we are meant to be. To some extent, therefore, shame is a spiritual power for good, mitigating the evil effect of the Fall. It is the influence of the Holy Spirit on our conscience, restraining us mercifully on the downward path of disobedience, and saving us from going utterly to the bad. Only when the sense of shame is deadened by vicious habits, its restorative power ceases.

Throughout the story of the Fall of our first parents, we trace a healing process of God's grace, even in the infliction of punishment. Man is sentenced to eat bread in the sweat of his face; but labour is a main condition of health and happiness.

> " If niggard Earth her treasures hide,
> To all but labouring hands denied,
> Lavish of thorns and worthless weeds alone ;
> The doom is half in mercy given,
> To train us in our way to Heaven,
> And show our lagging souls how glory must be won." [1]

To the woman it was said, "In sorrow shalt thou bring forth children:" but the seed of the woman was to bruise the serpent's head; and in general a mother's sorrow is turned into joy; so that the childless regard maternity as the happier lot.

A blessing underlies the awful sentence, "Thou shalt surely die." For the Saviour, revealed in the fulness of time, has taken the sting from death; and the faithful Christian

[1] "Christian Year."

soul is willing, perhaps even longing, "to depart and to be with Christ." The Tree of Life, though guarded by the flaming swords of Cherubim, is not shut out from hope. In the last book of the Bible we find the language of the first resumed, with the sentence of death revoked. We read again of Paradise and of the Tree of Life in the message of Christ to the Church of Ephesus. "To him that overcometh will I give to eat of the Tree of Life, which is in the midst of the Paradise of God."

There is also a hint of sacrificial atonement, according to the opinion of many theologians, in the brief record that the Lord God made coats of skins for Adam and Eve, and clothed them. These coats of skins have been supposed, not unreasonably, to indicate the slaying of beasts for sacrifice, as in later times, and to symbolize a robe of righteousness, given by God's mercy.

> "The very weeds we daily wear
> Are to Faith's eye a pledge of God's forgiving might."

Jewish teachers elaborated this idea with the fanciful minuteness peculiar to Rabbinical writings. But at all events, without going beyond the terms of Holy Scripture, we have a suggestion, if no more than a suggestion, of pardon through sacrifice, to be developed fully in the subsequent ordinances of the Old Covenant.

Thus the story of the Fall, in its obvious lessons, lays a foundation for the spiritual and moral instruction of mankind. Herein lies the chief importance of the early chapters of Genesis. To look to the Bible for physical knowledge is to mistake the purpose for which the Bible was given. Nature itself is the book in which God teaches knowledge of this kind, to the diligent inquirer. Holy men of old were inspired, not to trace the orbit of the stars, or calculate the age of the rocks, but to guide their brethren in the pilgrimage of daily life. For this end a revelation was given in simple childlike terms, to Moses or to the patriarchs before him. Milton, in his great poem, has represented Adam as learning from an angel the several steps of Creation; and on such speculative questions the insight of a poet is worth as much as that of a theologian. But the idea suggested by Hugh Miller, in his "Testimony of the Rocks," of a series of visions, commends itself to me more than any other on this abstruse subject.

In regard to the spiritual life of man, the Bible is full of lessons which correspond in some respects to the lessons of physical science. For instance, geologists find in the early strata organic forms which bear traces of affinity to forms of life now existing upon the earth, governed by the same laws of growth and decay which are at present in operation. Genesis shows us in like manner the early framework of the human soul. We trace in Adam the rudiments of the most vital features of our spiritual constitution. After the lapse of so many centuries before and after Christ, there remains in us the original character of our first parents. We, like them, desire naturally what is good for food, and pleasant to the eyes, and we desire to be made wise as God. We are tempted, as they were, to disobey God's law for our gratification; and we are punished, as they were, with justice tempered by mercy.

No part of the story is more suggestive of spiritual instruction than what is written concerning the Tree of Knowledge and the Tree of Life. For Knowledge and Life resemble two trees growing near to each other, so that their branches interlace, and their fruits intermingle. Perfect knowledge, the knowledge of God, is one with perfect life. "This is life eternal, to know Thee, the only true God, and Jesus Christ, whom Thou hast sent." But the unripe fruit of knowledge is often poisonous, and even the sweetest fruits turn to ashes, except under the conditions of obedience which God has ordained. Intellect, no less than appetite, has its measure and proportion among our faculties. By the confession of several who have sounded the depths of human knowledge apart from the fear of God, it leaves the mind hungry and weary of life. The author of Ecclesiastes is at one with the author of "Faust" in groaning over it all, as vanity and vexation of spirit; though the modern philosopher is less willing to accept the maxim "Fear God, and keep his commandments," as the sum of the whole matter. Culture of intellect at the cost of a reverential humble spirit, yields thorns and thistles to afflict the soul; and the ambition to "see life" as it is called, to be knowing in the mysteries of iniquity, is rarely gratified without moral degradation.

> "Woe to the man who seeks for truth by sin,
> Truth will to him be nevermore a joy."[1]

How knowledge and obedience can be reconciled, we learn from the example of Our Blessed Lord. In taking our nature upon Him, He underwent the several phases of human life from

[1] Schiller, "Das verschleierte Bild zu Sais."

infancy upward. He learned as a child, according to Isaiah's prophetic words, "to refuse the evil and choose the good." He increased in wisdom as He increased in stature. "Though he were a Son, yet learned He obedience by the things which He suffered," and He became subject to death, tasting death for every man. As disobedience drove the first Adam out of reach of the Tree of Life, so obedience regained the Tree of Life for the second Adam, and for His faithful servants.

In the present age there is a special need of the lesson of Adam's fall. For knowledge without reverence is a characteristic of the nineteenth century. There is a growing tendency to set knowledge in the place of religion, to assert or assume that knowledge is all that the soul requires for its perfection. In itself the increase of knowledge is a gain, but knowledge set in place of reverence, humility, purity, charity, knowledge which ignores God, is truly represented by the fruit of which our first parents partook to their sorrow.

From the triumphs of science we turn sadly to reflect on the moral corruption of great cities. While expeditions are fitted out to observe the transit of Venus from the southern hemisphere, and to dredge the ocean bed, the heart of our civilization is rotten for want of reverence for God's laws.

Adam was preserved in his fall from utter perdition by the sense of shame instilled into his conscience, by the discipline of toil for his daily bread, by the hope of final restoration. But it is possible to miss the good effect of all these remedial agencies. You may sear your conscience by familiar touch of evil, until you mock at sin, instead of blushing for shame. You may escape the wholesome discipline of labour, if you have the means of living in idleness. We are free to accept or reject the hope of salvation, which is offered in the Gospel of Christ. What then remains? Only to be judged according to our works—a terrible sentence in such a case.

Oh, that we might submit ourselves humbly to Christ's yoke, setting reverence and obedience above the gratification of bodily and mental desire!

> "Let knowledge grow from more to more,
> But more of reverence in us dwell;
> That mind and soul, according well,
> May make one music as before,
> But vaster."

Christ's yoke is easy and His burden is light,

when they are borne willingly; whereas the yoke of miscalled freedom presses heavily on the soul which holds it "free thinking" to be profane, and "free living" to be sensual. True freedom consists in allegiance to the true law of our nature, which subordinates our selfish wishes to our own enduring welfare, and to the order of God's kingdom. "The wages of sin is death." But the gates of Paradise are open, the Tree of Life bears imperishable fruit, and the harps and voices of Heaven sound welcome, to those who overcome the Tempter.

II. NOAH.

"By faith Noah, being warned of God of things not seen as yet, moved with fear, prepared an ark to the saving of his house."—*Hebrews*, xi. 7.

(Sexagesima, P.M.)

NOAH'S trust in God is one of the most illustrious examples of faith in the Bible, both for his rare virtue, standing alone in a wicked world, and also for the universal Deluge with which his name is associated. He appears in the records of Holy Scripture as a second founder of the human race, a type of the second Adam, who passed through the waters of Baptism, and through the very grave itself, as author of a new and regenerate life.

It is on the spiritual and moral significance of Noah's history that we can dwell most profitably. I think it is little more than waste of time in this place to investigate the questions of physical science which are connected with the Flood. Such questions, as to the manner of the Flood and its extent, are matters of curiosity, interesting in themselves, but apart from the consideration of the Flood as a moral lesson.

Our Lord refers to the Flood as a type of the Last Judgment. "As the days of Noah were, so shall the coming of the Son of Man be." He sets the Flood before us as a warning, in respect of the unprepared condition of the world when it came. St. Peter, who often speaks of the Flood, saw in it, not only a warning of future judgment, but a symbolical Baptism, a cleansing by water from sin to righteousness. And in the text another point is noted, the faith of the patriarch Noah, who believed God's word and acted on it, before the world had seen any such thing. These are the lessons which serve chiefly to apply the record of the Flood to our own conscience; and these lessons stand out clear and prominent in the midst of the obscurities of the Bible narrative. The judgment of the wicked and the salvation of God's people by grace through faith, are principles engraven on our memory by means of the record of the great Deluge. A world teeming with life is overwhelmed; a race of men already far advanced in mechanical and social arts, tilling the ground, working in metals, skilled in music, associated together in cities which they had learned to build, is utterly swept away. Noah, God's faithful servant, is preserved with his family from the waters which were the destruction of the ungodly; and not only from the waters, but by means of the waters, as St. Peter has observed. The Flood which purged the earth from sin, bore up the Ark in safety on its waves.

We can better appreciate these lessons by setting before ourselves in imagination, as vividly as we can, the principal scenes of the Deluge. Four sublime and terrible pictures comprise the sum of what is related in the Bible.

1. *The Antediluvian World.*

We have presented before us, in a few suggestive words, a tumult of selfishness and crime. Men are buying and selling, eating and drinking, marrying and giving in marriage, on the verge of utter destruction. Let us examine some of the details of the picture. There is before us, we may suppose, a merry group of feasters, entertained by the musical instruments of the sons of Jubal. Yonder is a triumph of one of the mighty men of the time: for there were "mighty men," "men of renown," in those days, although their name and fame have perished, without any monument to record them.

Further on we may see in fancy an affrighted crowd, scared by some deed of violence of the ancient giants; for "there were giants in the earth in those days;" and "the earth was filled with violence." In the distance are the tents and flocks of the peaceful herdsmen of Seth's posterity and the walled cities of the sons of Cain. Far and near God's all-seeing eye was over them as it is described in the xivth Psalm: "The Lord looked down from heaven upon the children of men; to see if there were any that would understand, and seek after God. But they are all gone out of the way, they are altogether become abominable: there is none that doeth good, no, not one."

Yet there is among them a preacher of righteousness, who has been inspired to foresee the coming judgment, and who bears witness to his faith in deeds more emphatic than words. He has just brought to completion the long labour of the Ark. The huge vessel has risen up in the sight of all men for a testimony to God's word, every blow of the hammer serving to proclaim the builder's faith. Now it stands ready for launching, but with no preparations for a launch, though many for a voyage. The freight of animals ordained to preserve their kind is already collected, and provision has been made for a twelvemonth's food.

The world goes its way, taking no notice of these things. Yet above, in the sky, is an ominous writing, if any had eyes to discern it: a gathering of clouds, piled up higher and higher in airy castles, and blotting out the sun: a fearful shudder of the foliage on every tree with the disquietude of rising tempest, a cowering of dumb animals with instinctive terror before the storm,—

> " For beast and bird have seen and heard
> That which man knoweth not."

This is what we have reason to imagine of the moment before the Flood began. Let us pass on to another picture.

2. *The beginning of the Flood.*

We read of the fountains of the great deep broken up, and the windows of heaven opened. That is, there is a two-fold deluge. Not only is the earth flooded by rains which overflow every lake and river, but a vast tidal wave sweeps in from the ocean, from the "fountains of the great deep." Each spot of rising ground is the refuge of a bewildered multitude drawn together by the common danger. Man and beast, friend and enemy, the fiercest and the most timid, huddle together with no other thought but that of escaping death. In that hour of mortal fear each clings to the object which is most precious. The selfish think only of self-preservation, but the more kindly affections of nature are shown even in extremity. The mother still holds fast her child at peril of her own life. The brave dies bravely, the coward like a coward. Meanwhile the large form of the Ark looms indistinctly through the torrent of rain, visible yet inaccessible. Noah and his family are there shut in, and they who had mocked them recently would now give all they possess to join their company. But it is too late.

"The day of grace is past and gone."

The details of this picture are too horrible for imagination to contemplate minutely, as the rising waters engulf first one and then another of the groups of survivors. We must pass away from this scene to glance for a moment at a third picture.

3. *The Flood at its Height.*

Nothing is to be seen now, except the Ark

floating alone on a boundless expanse of water. Where lately had been a busy and populous world, there is now a sea without a shore, so far as the eye can range. How far we cannot determine, and need not inquire; but the traditions of nations as far as possible removed from Noah (the American Indians, for instance) are so much in harmony, that they tend to confirm the ancient belief that the dispersion of mankind took place after the Flood, and that the Flood was at least co-extensive with the race of man. What we are told is apparently related from the point of view of those who were saved, Noah and his family. We read that " the high hills under the whole heaven" are covered. It is impossible, therefore, to tell where the land is, except by sounding, and this is what Noah seems actually to have done. We are told, " Fifteen cubits upward did the waters prevail." This measure of depth, which can only have been taken from the Ark, since there was no other point of observation within reach, sets before us the experience of the patriarch in the midst of desolation. As the Ark floats high over plains and cities, valleys and hills, this is the only point at which he becomes aware of ground beneath him. Landmarks were all gone. Water was everywhere—above, around, beneath—except that at one point, five fathoms below, he touched with his line the solid earth, and that at some unknown spot.

From this scene of desolation let us turn to another and brighter picture.

4. *The New World.*

The rain has ceased, and the flood subsided. The Ark leans, stranded, on the mountain side of Ararat, and the inmates come forth rejoicing into the sunshine from their long imprisonment. The raven has flown away to feast, according to his nature, on the dead; the dove has returned with a leaf of olive, a sign of renewed vegetation. Noah, surrounded by his family, offers a sacrifice to the Lord God with a thankful heart, while high overhead the great bow of heaven spans the sky as a pledge of God's covenant; and along the mountain slopes, and far down into the distance, the new shoots of spring display themselves, a spring such as the world had never known.

But our interest centres on that family group. Their sacrifice is the great primal example of Family Prayer. It is a sacrifice of thanksgiving for past mercies, a solemn act of faith in God's providential care, and an act of communion with Him by the offering of blood, a type of the sacrifice of the Lamb that was to be slain in due time on earth, and that had been slain in the Divine Counsels before the foundation of the world. Noah's sacrifice was, on the one hand, a foreshadowing of that which we commemorate in the Sacrament of the Body and Blood of Christ; and, on the other hand, it illustrated that sacred bond of worship which unites father and child, brother and sister, in religious service as members of a family. Doubtless family worship was observed by the older patriarchs before the Flood; but it is on this occasion that it receives distinct mention in Holy Scripture. Thus every act of worship, the most solemn and the most domestic, comes down to us by inheritance from that ancient pattern of sacrifice, by which Noah inaugurated the second period of the human race.

Not only this, however, but every portion of the story of the Flood is invested with significant meaning for us. We are told in Scripture, again and again, with the most urgent admonition, to look forward to such another Day of Judgment, in which not Water, but Fire, shall be God's agent of destruction. "The heavens being on fire shall be dissolved, and the elements shall melt with fervent heat." And when that fiery flood is past, the spiritual Ark of God, the Church of Christ, will be exalted to the top of the hills, according to the visions of the prophets and the Apocalypse of St. John. We may trace an allusion to the Flood when St. John writes: "I saw a new heaven and a new earth, for the first heaven and the first earth were passed away; and there was no more sea." Again, when he saw in the spirit a great and high mountain, and the heavenly city descending on it, there is a notable correspondence to the Ark resting with its sacred freight upon Ararat.

The destruction of the old world, with all its accessories, concerns us practically with reference to the future. Who can say when the doom of the present world, so long predicted, will be fulfilled? Shall we doubt the prediction because it speaks of "things not seen as yet"? That is what the antediluvians did, to their destruction. Shall we wait for clearer signs of the times? If those signs were much clearer than they are, it would be too late to begin providing for our salvation.

Noah's example of faith is instructive in

several respects. It was far-sighted, confident, steadfast, practical. He applied himself soberly to a work of great labour, preparing an Ark to the saving of his house. While he had faith to expect the Deluge, he had also faith to persevere without haste in his work, accomplishing it by little and little. Want of faith is shown sometimes by mere incredulity, sometimes by a timid and anxious impatience. Thus it is not an uncommon thing for the same persons who have lived carelessly, without thought or fear of God, to be moved in times of excitement by panic fear, passing at once from irreligious want of faith to superstitious want of faith; that is, to a spasmodic devotion which has little genuine trust in God. For such persons the example of the patriarch Noah is specially appropriate.

Moreover, for all of us, the work of faith at which we are called to labour is in some respects like Noah's. We have to take part in the building of an Ark—namely, that fabric which the Ark typifies, the Church of our Saviour Jesus Christ. This figure, which is made familiar to us in the Baptismal Service, where we say "the Ark of Christ's Church," has a fuller meaning when we look forward to the consummation of all things, to that final completion of the Church in which we are called to be fellow-workers with God. Every one of us is called to take part in building up the mystical Ark, as God has given us grace. The wood of which it is formed is the wood of the Cross. When Christ bids us take up the Cross and follow Him, He calls us to the service by which in truth the spiritual structure of His Church is fabricated. How in this Ark all races of men are to be received, with other analogies, has been drawn out at length by Augustine and some early Fathers.[1] We have the Lord Jesus Christ for our Master-Builder, under whom various offices are assigned to us severally. To one the interpretation of God's Word, to another the instruction of the ignorant, to another the exhortation of the careless, to another the relief of sickness or distress, to another the social influence which binds neighbours together in Christian fellowship. All these diversities of administrations are guided by the same Spirit, and they serve in their respective modes to the edification of the Church.

Finally, our work must be done in reverence and in faith: in godly fear of our Lord's dis-

---

[1] De Civitate Dei, xv. 27, etc.

pleasure, and in faith that He is just and merciful. The trial of fire awaits us and our work. But the fire is a minister of judgment in the hands of a righteous God, a fire which, while it destroys the evil, purifies the good. "He is like a refiner's fire."

III. ABRAHAM.

"Now the Lord had said unto Abram, Get thee out of thy country, and from thy kindred, and from thy father's house, unto a land that I will shew thee."—*Genesis* xii. 1.

(Quinquagesima, P.M.)

WE are introduced in these words to the history of that great patriarch, who was to be known for all future ages as the Father of the Faithful. What we read of him, before we become acquainted with his character, is that he migrated from his home, leaving his kindred behind, and after many journeys found a new home in another land. This migration of his, we are told, was at the Lord's bidding. His own wish in the matter was governed by an inspiration of the Lord Jehovah, who said to him, "Get thee out of thy country, and from thy kindred, and from thy father's house, unto a land that I will show thee."

If we take a wide survey of the history of the world, we shall observe that Abraham's example, though illustrious beyond others, does not stand alone. At certain periods, with long intervals between, there has sprung up a restless spirit of movement among men, they know not how. It has come to pass on a sudden that large tribes and even nations have felt themselves impelled to strike their tents, to put their flocks and herds in motion, and to migrate to some new land, previously unvisited. There is much reason to suppose that the passage of Abraham into Canaan was part of a more extensive migration westward of the pastoral tribes of Chaldæa. The hieroglyphic inscriptions of Egypt have been so far deciphered as to record a great invasion of Shepherd-Kings about this period: and we have a confirmation of the fact in the list of nations mentioned in Scripture as bordering on the Holy Land: Moabites, Ammonites, Midianites, Edomites, Ishmaelites, all tracing their descent from the family stock of Abraham, and leaving their home in Ur of the Chaldees.

Of similar national migrations, the most notable took place about two thousand years later. When the Empire of Ancient Rome began to decay, there came an incursion of tribes from the north, rushing onward like the successive waves of a stormy sea when the tide is rising. Goths and Huns, Vandals and Lombards, followed one another tumultuously, each impelled by an invisible power which had its origin in God's will. Secondary causes no doubt there were, but so far as human eyes could discern, that vast movement of nations was spontaneous. It was as when a frozen river melts, and the packed ice is borne impetuously down the stream. The normal state of mankind over vast regions changed from a state of rest to a state of motion. Men rose up, day by day, equipped for a journey, no longer accounting any place their settled habitation. By degrees this human deluge subsided, not until many centuries had elapsed: and, strange to say, the restlessness of the northern races found its limit on the shores of the same Holy Land where the eastern race of Abraham had found a home. The Crusades mark the close of a period of wandering, to be followed by a period of comparative rest.

Yet now once more, within the memory of young men, a new mysterious impulse of movement seems to spread itself over the face of the whole earth. Almost every nation is stirred more or less by the influence of this spirit, but it is felt most of all in Great Britain. We may reckon in our own acquaintance families, in which one member has gone to the far East, another to the far West. One, it may be, is keeping sheep, like Jacob, on the wide pastures of an Australian colony; another, like Esau, is leading the life of a hunter, in American forests; another, like Joseph, is giving prudent counsel, at the court of some Asiatic prince. Such is the spirit of the age; and though we can trace the effect upward a little way towards the source, we must acknowledge a Divine power at the fountain-head. It is the breath of God which has set the nations in movement, as the summer sun, shining upon the Alps, thaws the snow fields and fills the mountain torrents.

The restless love of movement is chiefly shown in emigration. We have only to compare a recent map of North America with one of half a century ago, to see the enormous movement of our race to the West. There, above all, it appears as if the Lord had said to our brethren, "Get thee out of thy country, and from thy kindred, and from thy father's house, unto a land that I will show thee." But the westerly tide of emigration is only one of many. It spreads in all directions and cannot be restrained. Our rulers have endeavoured in vain to set limits to its progress, warning men that if they cross certain frontiers, they do so at their own peril. Intrepid men are still found crossing the border, either for adventure, or else in the nobler cause of humanity; and thus we find ourselves drawn by a strong chain of sympathy to lands more and more remote. A few years since, the public interest in a heroic Missionary prompted an expedition, which opened to the world the resources of the Zambese and the Congo. And more lately the manhood of Great Britain was hastening in the track of another hero, to unexplored regions of the Nile.

Nearer home, and on a smaller scale, the national movement of which I speak is illustrated by the English colonies which have been formed on the Mediteranean, as winter resorts for invalids. Altogether, the habit of foreign travel, both for business and for pleasure, shows the same disposition. It used to be said formerly that men travelled to learn languages or for some other studious purpose. But this is really the exception, not the rule. Travelling has become a fashion. Men scale difficult mountains, and cross deserts, undergoing the extremity of hunger and thirst, not so much for gain, or for any definite good to be accomplished, as for a desire urging them on, forbidding them to be still. There is in the air a passionate spirit of inquiry, which leaves no stone unturned, if it may possibly hide some fragment of an inscription, some unfamiliar plant, or reptile, or fossil, however insignificant. Besides, there is a modern sentiment of fellowship with Nature, a contemplative mood which delights to observe the sublime beauties of mountain, cloud, and sea, in their varied aspects; so that scenes which used to be the terror of travellers in former times are now the chosen haunts of tourists. There is also a spirit of human brotherhood, which rejoices in breaking down the barriers of language and custom, and in learning to recognize man as man under a foreign garb. While motives like these actuate the more intelligent sort of travellers, there is a crowd who follow the fashion blindly, treading in the steps of their fellow-countrymen, and so much attached to the usages of their life at home, that change of place brings to them no change of mind.

The modern parallels to which I have referred may serve, perhaps, to throw a fresh light on the story of the migration of Abraham, and to associate with it some practical lessons. Whether the spirit of movement be shown in emigration, or in voyages undertaken for commerce, or in foreign travel, I have no doubt that it is a vital force which God has given, and which has a good use. God's gifts are open to be used well or ill, by those to whom He entrusts them. When we say that God causes the wind to blow, that does not mean that He bids us to sail in the direction of the wind; it is a power from God which brings welfare to the wise, and calamity to the foolish. So also the restless spirit of inquiry and adventure, which impels men to leave their home, is for good or evil, according to the control which is applied to it. There is a quaint wisdom, worth laying to heart, in the saying of an old writer, that travellers are like the ships of Solomon's fleet, as mentioned 1 Chronicles ix. "Some bring home gold and silver; others bring home peacocks and apes." It rests with each whether he brings home solid treasure from experience of foreign lands; or whether he has nothing to show but self-conceit and a degraded manhood. There are certain advantages which accompany foreign travels, and also certain dangers. It is well to set both before our eyes. Although the impulse to leave home may be at first a blind impulse, like the instinct which drives the young bird from its nest, the subsequent effect must be greatly determined for better or worse by the objects which we propose to ourselves, and the turn which we give to our thoughts.

The advantages of travel, speaking not from a commercial or political point of view, but from a spiritual point of view, may be summed up under two heads. Experience of foreign countries enlarges our view, first, of the universal Fatherhood of God, and, secondly, of the universal Brotherhood of mankind. To a reverent mind those truths are deeply impressed by what we see and hear abroad. Narrow, partisan, and selfish ideas of every kind give way under experience of institutions and societies unlike our own. We learn to recognize the God of our fathers as God of all the earth, the Maker and Preserver of everything that lives, the Ruler of the winds and the sea. Thus it is said by the Psalmist :—

> "They that go down to the sea in ships,
> And occupy their business in great waters,
> These men see the works of the Lord,
> And His wonders in the deep."

And so many a lonely traveller, far from home,

wakes up to a sense of God's fatherly care such as Abraham and Jacob and Joseph felt. When separated from friends and from the forms of public worship which we have cherished as means of communion with God, we learn to understand that even in the wilderness there is a way from earth to heaven, like the ladder of Jacob's vision. The all-powerful mediation of Christ gains a new importance for us.

Secondly, experience of foreign countries teaches us the brotherhood of mankind. The dullest and most heedless of observers cannot but feel the kinship of his fellow-men more for associating with them. Natural prejudices of race and manners melt away with more intimate acquaintance, and thus travel prepares us to realize the great truths, that God has "made of one blood all nations of men," and that in Christ "There is neither Greek nor Jew, circumcision nor uncircumcision, Barbarian, Scythian, bond or free: but Christ is all and in all." Travel gives a largeness of mind, which the Holy Spirit develops to a more extended Christian charity than is bred in the circle of home life; and this enlargement of mind has also the effect of raising us above petty aims and sordid cares, to a more generous view of things.

These are some of the advantages to be gained by foreign travel. On the other hand there are dangers, both numerous and manifest. We have an instance in the history of Abraham in Egypt, where he was found guilty of a base deception at the court of Pharaoh. Elsewhere he was the most magnanimous of men, but there he seemed to lose the dignity of his character. So to this day, under the seductive influence of foreign cities, men are tempted to forget God's presence, as if they were heathens and had left their gods behind them. Another danger is selfishness. Those who voluntarily break the ties of home to dwell among strangers, may be moved by God's Spirit to form new ties in their adopted home. But if they form no fresh ties, and take to wandering to and fro in self-indulgent luxury, wherever climate or scenery or society is most delightful, they become hardhearted.

We are hardly aware to what extent we are upheld, both in religion and in virtue, by the pressure of public opinion around us. A man dares not, for shame, set at nought the praise and blame of his neighbours, if they are neighbours among whom he has to spend his life. He may at heart be irreligious, but he conforms to the religion of his country; he may at heart be immoral, but he behaves himself so as not to cause scandal; and the habit of doing right becomes a second nature, so long as he remains at home. All this is changed when he goes abroad. There, moving from place to place at will, he need not care what his neighbours think of him. He will find among foreigners a standard of right and wrong different in many respects to that of his fellow-countrymen. Under such circumstances the principles which are founded on mere custom give way, and a man's soul is exposed unprotected to all the temptations of the world, the flesh, and the devil. Experience of foreign travel is thus a test of the good and the bad in us. Sound faith is strengthened: weak faith which has no root is withered away.

Let us refer again to the history of the patriarch Abraham for a practical lesson. It is related of him that when he came to a resting-place at Bethel and at Hebron, "he built an altar to the Lord, and called on the name of the Lord." By the reverent acknowledgment of God's presence, and the offering of sacrifice to Him, he set God always before his face. Following in his steps three generations later,

Joseph was enabled to remember in Egypt that God was with him. Those who dwell in foreign lands, and especially among the heathen, have peculiar need of daily prayer, united or private. By frequent communing in spirit with the Lord Jesus Christ, even if outward means of grace be wanting, we shall be guarded by His constant fellowship. The Eternal God will be with us, Father, Son and Holy Ghost, like the three Angels who visited Abraham under the tree at Mamre, and condescended to his repast, and showered blessings on him and his posterity.

IV. ISAAC.

"Thou shalt go unto my country, and to my kindred, and take a wife for my son Isaac."—*Genesis* xxiv. 4.

AT a very solemn moment in the Marriage Service the names of Isaac and Rebekah are mentioned as examples of faithful wedlock. Immediately before joining the hands of the bride and bridegroom, the Minister prays, "that as Isaac and Rebekah lived faithfully together, so these persons may surely perform and keep the vow and covenant betwixt them made." Inquiring minds have often wondered what there is in Holy Scripture to distinguish them from others; and those who call to mind the deceit which was practised on Isaac in his blind old age by Rebekah, desire a higher standard of conjugal fidelity. Yet the divines who drew up our Prayer Book knew the Bible at least as well as we do; and it cannot be doubted that they saw good reason for the choice of Isaac and Rebekah among patriarchal names, notwithstanding the great fault, which is so exactly recorded and was so severely punished.

The key to this, as to many difficulties which meet us in Scripture, when we are invited to take for examples the men and women of old time, is the gradual unfolding, or evolution, of God's law in the history of the world. There is a growth in the human race, as in an individual man, from infancy to adult age. What we read in Genesis is the infancy of mankind. And Isaac is the earliest of the patriarchs whose life presents to us a picture of the union of husband and wife at all closely resembling that of Christian matrimony. We refer to him as the most ancient, not as the most perfect; just as in museums we value the flint implements, which tell of primitive races long since vanished, more than the cutlery of Sheffield.

Let us cast our eyes back for a little to the early chapters of human history, in which the brief record of Genesis is supplemented by traditions of various nations, and by the relics found in caverns and elsewhere. It is plain that the old world had in general little idea of that holy bond of matrimony which unites for better or worse two lives in one. Not Abraham, nor Jacob, nor Esau, understood marriage as we understand it. In their day, as even now in the East, the patriarchs knew no law to restrain them from taking several wives. A higher ideal of family life came gradually and slowly to have the force of a moral law, and in the New Testament was established by the authoritative sanction of the Holy Spirit. That a man should have more than one wife has been forbidden in the Christian Church from the beginning. But this law marks an advance beyond the custom of the patriarchs and of the most illustrious of the Kings of Israel; for instance, David and Solomon. Thus, the marriage of Isaac and Rebekah stands out conspicuously as an early example worthy of remembrance.

The description of the betrothal of Isaac forms one of the most interesting pictures in the Bible. It is a beautiful idyll of patriarchal life, touching in its earnest simplicity. Abraham in his old age, soon after Sarah's death, desires to see his son Isaac married, and not to a woman of the Canaanites among whom he dwelt. He therefore sends his chief retainer, Eliezer, to Mesopotamia, to find a wife for Isaac of his own kindred, the family of Nahor. At the same time he lays a strict charge upon him, that Isaac is not to return thither again. So Eliezer takes with him ten camels loaded with presents, and when he arrives at Haran, he rests his camels by a well outside the city. There he prays to the God of Abraham, the Lord Jehovah, to prosper his journey. "O Lord God of my master Abraham, I pray thee, send me good speed this day, and show kindness unto my master Abraham. Behold, I stand here by the well of water; and the daughters of the men of the city come out to draw water: and let it come to pass, that the damsel to whom I shall say, Let down thy pitcher, I pray thee, that I may drink; and she shall say, Drink, and I will give thy camels drink also: let the same be she that thou hast appointed for thy servant Isaac; and thereby shall I know that thou hast shewed kindness unto my master."

Before he had done speaking, his prayer was answered. Rebekah, daughter of Bethuel, the son of Abraham's brother Nahor, came out with a pitcher upon her shoulder, a maiden of fair countenance, and Eliezer's heart rose hopefully at the sight of her. He ran to meet her, and said, "Give me to drink, I pray thee, a little water of thy pitcher." And she replied at once, "Drink, my lord;" and after giving him drink, she offered to draw water for his camels. So she poured the contents of the pitcher into the trough, and made haste to draw more, until the camels had done drinking. By the fulfilment of the sign which he had prayed for, he trusted that God's providence had guided him to the object of his journey. While the camels were drinking, he looked at her in silence and amazement. Then he took out a golden ring and two bracelets and gave them to her, asking whose daughter she was, and if he could have lodging at her father's house. She told him her name, and said there was room for him and for the camels. Thereupon she ran home to prepare for him, and presently her brother Laban came to bid him welcome. He came, thanking God for prospering him so far as to guide him to the house of his master's brother; but he refused to eat until he had told his errand. Laban and his father, Bethuel, who seems to have been infirm, as he bears a secondary part, heard the man's tale to the end and said, "The thing proceeds from the Lord: we cannot speak unto thee bad or good. Rebekah is before thee, take her, and go, and let her be thy master's son's wife, as the Lord hath spoken." Eliezer bowed himself to the earth in thankfulness to God. He brought out more presents, silver and gold, and raiment, and on the morrow he asked leave to return home with the damsel. They would have kept her for a few days, but he pressed his suit, and it was left for Rebekah herself to decide. She said, "I will go," and went back with Eliezer, accompanied by her nurse and other attendants. As they drew near to Abraham's dwelling-place, at evening, Isaac was at prayer, and when he lifted his eyes he saw them approaching. Rebekah asked Eliezer, "What man is this?" And he said, "It is my master." So she alighted from the camel and covered herself with a veil, as was customary for brides before marriage in their husband's presence. Then Isaac led her to his mother's tent, and "she became his wife, and he loved her, and Isaac was comforted after his mother's death."

In the simple grace of this story we have an explanation of the tenderness with which the names of Isaac and Rebekah are cited in the Prayer Book as examples of married life. We strengthen the sacred bonds of society when we connect our modern life with the beginnings, the ancient roots, from which all that is purest and best in our social condition proceeds. An American visitor to England, the philosopher

Emerson, relates with sympathy how he heard this chapter of Genesis read in York Minster, on the day of the enthroning of the Archbishop, as it happened to be the evening lesson. Our reverence for the Scriptures impressed his critical mind as an element of civilization, which was important to the well-being of the English people, "binding old and new."

Comparing the espousals of Isaac and Rebekah with a modern engagement of marriage, we cannot but observe how little the principal persons exercised a choice of their own in the matter. One of the chief points of difference between ancient and modern manners is, that formerly each individual took a place as member of a family, in subordination to his or her elders. Even the heir, as long as he was no more than an heir, differed little from a servant, although he was the future lord. Isaac submits to his father's will, which is that the confidential servant of the family should choose a wife for him, not among his alien neighbours, but among the daughters of his father's kinsmen in Mesopotamia. Rebekah accepts the decision of her brother and father, and goes cheerfully to a new home, in obedience to what seems the will of God, to become the wife of a man whom she has never seen. On both sides, but especially on that of the gentle Isaac, we see a habit of obedience to the laws of family duty, which is nowadays almost forgotten. The spirit of loyalty in every form is just now out of fashion. As young men and young women grow up to maturity they repudiate the claims of their family, and assert their own individual rights. They, like their predecessors of old time, have known the blessings of a father's and mother's care. They have been watched through anxious days and nights in infancy; they have been carefully nursed through the maladies of childhood; they have been fed, clothed, educated, until they came to an age to "do their own," as we say in Lancashire; that is, to shift for themselves.

What of that? The power to be independent makes free to cancel all obligations, to disown the ties of nature and of gratitude, and to set at nought the commandment and the promise, "Honour thy father and thy mother, that thy days may be long in the land which the Lord thy God giveth thee."

I do not say that we should go back to the primitive simplicity of the patriarchal age; for I believe that progress is God's law, and that the due assertion of individual character is a step in advance, in social relations. But I am sure that ungrateful and unfilial conduct is not blessed by God, and that it is the special danger of these times to think of rights more than duties, and to overlook real duties while clamouring for imaginary rights.

This, at all events, may be said in favour of the manners of the early ages of the world, compared with our own. When young men and maidens contracted the sacred bond of marriage in a spirit of obedience to the judgment of their elders, they were more likely to be loyal to the new obligation in proportion to their fidelity to the old. On the other hand, the self-will, which insists on a free choice without regard to parents, is a bad security for faithfulness to the pledges of matrimony. A selfish son is apt to prove a selfish husband, a selfish daughter to prove a selfish wife. The independence of character, which overrides the claims of filial duty to gratify one passion, may too easily override the most solemn vows to gratify another. We know but little of the married life of Isaac and Rebekah. They were happy, in that there is no history of the many years that intervened between their youth and their old age.

"Along the cool sequester'd vale of life
They kept the noiseless tenour of their way."

But the evening of their days is disclosed to us in a well-known chapter, so vivid and so true to human nature, that we cannot but pause to reflect upon it. Isaac has grown old and fond of savoury meat; and his eyes are dim, that he cannot see. Rebekah likewise has grown old. The chief interest of both is no longer in each other, but in their children. Each has a favourite. The mild father is partial to the adventurous hunter, Esau, his first-born. The mother loves best her home-keeping son, Jacob. Her partiality leads her to a guilty deceit, for which she pays the penalty of losing the company of Jacob for the remainder of her life, and being vexed to the weariness of her soul by the daughters of Heth, whom Esau brought home to be members of her family.

The picture is a sorrowful one, not the less for being a life-like representation of many a household of our own day. If the tenderness of early affection passes away, as husband and wife grow old, if their hearts are turned from each other to their children, and with unfair partiality to one in particular, there is likely to follow a disloyal practice of deception, the mother taking advantage of the father's ignorance, his love of good cheer, or any other weakness, to help or screen her favourite.

Sad that the life-long fellowship, begun with the plighted vows of bride and bridegroom, should ever come to this! That it may not be so, the blessing of Christ, invoked in holy matrimony, should be sought continually. Nothing but His all-powerful grace can sustain our good resolutions through the wear and tear of life. The love which is based on admiration of youthful beauty soon must fade; the love which is based on congenial tastes and habits will cool; the love which sets children in the first place will sometimes wreck their happiness, by weakening the husband's authority. The one sure ground which cannot fail is love which is yielded first to Christ, and then to each other as members of Christ. Such love, if it undergo some shocks and storms in the voyage of life, takes refuge in Christ's more immediate presence as in a harbour, where shattered mast and torn sail may be repaired. At the Lord's Altar, or in united prayer at home, hearts which have been for a while put out of harmony learn to reconcile their discords, that the music of wedded life may be restored. And thus in many a plain Christian family the bond of holy matrimony will be more sacred, and mutual love more enduring, than in the tents of that ancient patriarch whose life is both an example and a warning to us.

V. ESAU.

"Esau, who for one morsel of meat sold his birthright."
—*Hebrews* xii. 16.

OUR Lord's parable, in which he likens the kingdom of heaven to treasure hid in a field, suggests the comparison of Holy Scripture to a document in cypher revealing the secret of the hidden treasure. Such a paper must be studied carefully, to be interpreted rightly; for its directions will mislead those who use them without care. And so also the lessons of the Bible, which point the way to the hidden riches of spiritual truth, require patience on our part to understand and apply them.

Of this we have an instance in the history of Esau, whose character is more apt to be misjudged than that of any other of the patriarchs. God's disapproval of him leads many superficial readers of the Bible to set him down simply as wicked, without observing in what his wickedness consists, or in what his example is an instructive warning. On the other hand, readers who look at Esau's character by the light of nature are disposed at first sight to take his part, seeing in him a bold, generous manliness which contrasts favourably in many respects with the cunning of the brother who supplanted him. Unless we look below the surface, we shall hardly reconcile the judgment of our conscience with that Divine Voice which said, "Jacob have I loved, and Esau have I hated."

Yet one word of the Epistle to the Hebrews gives the key to this difficult question. Esau is there called "a profane person," and following the train of thought which that word "profane" suggests, we can do justice to the better features of his character, and nevertheless recognize his unworthiness to be heir to the blessing of Abraham and Isaac.

Profane is the opposite of sacred. As a personal quality it means, to be without that religious sensibility which is the first element of spiritual life. A profane person is without awe or reverence for God, and pays no respect to things which are hallowed by association with God, such as holy names, holy places, holy seasons. As to these things it sometimes happens, though rarely, that good men are indifferent to them out of fulness of spiritual life, which is conscious of God's presence at all times and places alike. To the holy all things are holy, but to the profane nothing is holy. The religious feeling which moves the angels to veil their faces before God's glorious presence, is a feeling of which they are insensible, unless it be to laugh at it in others.

With this great sin of profaneness Esau stands charged in the Epistle to the Hebrews. Let us see how the charge is borne out by his conduct as recorded in the Old Testament, Genesis xxv. Esau came from hunting, faint and hungry, to the place where Jacob was, and begged a meal of pottage. " Jacob said, Sell me this day thy birthright. And Esau said, Behold I am at the point to die; and what profit shall this birthright do me? And Jacob said, Swear to me this day: and he sware unto him; and he sold his birthright unto Jacob. Then Jacob gave Esau bread and pottage of lentiles; and he did eat and drink, and rose up, and went his way: thus Esau despised his birthright."

In reading this story we cannot but be indignant at the selfish craft of Jacob. Doubtless our indignation is right, and drawn from a higher and purer source than the patriarchs attained to. Moreover, Jacob's faults are faults peculiarly repugnant to our race and nation. God has endowed Englishmen with a love of truth and fair dealing, which is wanting in general to the nations of the East. Of the two great instruments of human wrong, force and fraud, our nation is inclined to the former rather than the latter. We judge sins of violence more leniently than sins of cunning. Thus we are predisposed to blame Jacob not only with a just, but with an excessive severity. How Jacob's sins received their due punishment from the chastening hand of God is one of the most instructive lessons in the Bible. But our present subject is not the character of Jacob, but of Esau.

What is remarkable in the description of Esau's sale of his birthright, is the indifference with which he gave it up. "Thus Esau despised his birthright" is the reflection which sums up the whole. We have therefore to consider what his birthright was, for on this everything turns. The first-born of a patriarchal family had rights of which only a faint trace is preserved in modern institutions. He was absolute head of the tribe. In him were combined the most sacred of the attributes which in later times were assigned to distinct persons or orders. The offering of sacrifice to God, the power of government and military command, the offices, in short, of priest and king, were united in the patriarchs. Sometimes it was the prerogative of the first-born to transmit his name to his descendants as the representative name of a people. So Ishmael and Esau himself gave names to future nations. But the birthright had a special sacredness in the line of Abraham and Isaac; for the blessing of the covenant presumably went along with it. To Abraham and Isaac it had been said, "In thee and in thy seed shall all the families of the earth be blessed."

Now, in the course of nature, the same promise was the expected inheritance of Isaac's first-born; and this is what Esau gave up for a meal; namely, that the Lord God should be called the God of Jacob rather than the God of Esau; that Israel, not Edom, should be the name of God's chosen people; that his brother's name, not his own, should be associated for ever with the Incarnation of the Saviour of the world, and with the spiritual glories of the kingdom of Heaven.[1]

Esau could not foresee all this. We never can foresee the remote consequences of our actions. But the profane levity which made

---

[1] See Numb. vii., 1 Chron. v., Gen. xxviii., 14.

him hold his birthright cheap, proved his unworthiness. We must not suppose him to be less responsible for his conduct, because of the words of God which had declared " The elder shall serve the younger." God's predestination is never to be understood in a sense which would abrogate man's freedom and moral duty.

As for Esau's plea "I am at the point to die," it has every appearance of being a gross exaggeration of his sense of hunger and fatigue. Were it otherwise, we should not be told that he despised his birthright. His character, the character of a profane man, is vividly expressed in the question, "What profit shall this birthright do me?" Not so have honourable men regarded their sacred privileges.

Among the legends of ancient Rome is one which throws light, by contrast, on the sin of Esau. The city was closely besieged by the Gauls: and on a certain day it was the custom of one of the great families to offer sacrifice in a temple outside the city, which was in the enemy's hands. To make this solemn offering was the birthright of the head of the family. When the day came round, he put on his sacrificial robes, and went forth at the peril of apparently certain death, into the midst of the enemy; but not to perish. The barbarians were awed by the conduct of one who valued his birthright more than life, and made way for him to go and return again.[1]

Indeed, brethren, if we permit ourselves to balance between life and honour, there is little hope of honour remaining to us. If we ask in moments of temptation, "What profit shall this birthright do me?" the flesh is always at hand to urge its immediate wants above the hope of things unseen. Unless we feel the supreme authority of that voice of the Spirit within us, which sets honour and virtue above earthly comfort, we can give no adequate reply to the question, "What profit shall it do me?" Honour is nothing if it is not supreme. All spiritual good, weighed by material standards, appears light in the balance. It requires a spiritual faculty to discern the treasures of the unseen world.

In this respect we see the ground of preference for Jacob, with all his faults, over Esau. Jacob lived by faith. The presence of the God of his fathers was felt by him throughout his lifelong pilgrimage. Visions of angels hovered about his path and about his bed. When we

[1] Livy, v. 46. Smith, Dict. Antiq. "Gens," "Sacra."

read of these, we must remember that celestial visions are only for those who have eyes to see. The perception of the spiritual world, which is not far from any one of us, is given only to souls which are duly qualified; as the sun-pictures are formed only on duly prepared paper. Jacob by force of his faith in the unseen, his indomitable patience and perseverance in looking to blessings afar off, stands altogether upon a higher level of humanity than his brother. The difference between them is like the difference between the race of man and the highest of the brute creation. Men like Esau, brave and good-natured, according to what is termed good-nature, but living merely in the present, have the glory which belongs to a noble work of God's animal kingdom, a little higher than the beasts which he pursues. His pleasure is in his field sports, his armed retainers, his heathen wives: he eats and drinks to-day, for to-morrow he dies, and he has no care beyond. Whatever progress has been made by mankind in the lapse of ages has been made, under God's providence, by men of Jacob's stamp. Such men, far-sighted and filled by a great idea, have discovered and peopled America, invented the printing-press and the steam-engine, and other great instruments of civilization. Such men built up great cities and empires on the sandbanks of Venice and in the swamps of Holland. In the history of the rise of the Dutch Republic we have many noble instances of a choice the contrary to that of Esau: endurance of the utmost extremity of famine rather than forego the birthright of religious liberty.

That birthright which Esau forfeited is, in a spiritual sense, the inheritance of every one of us. As Christians, we are heirs of the promises made to Abraham, by the right of our new birth in the kingdom of Christ. We are made Kings and Priests according to the testimony of St. Peter and St. John: Kings, that we may reign with Christ; Priests, that we may offer spiritual sacrifices to God in Christ. Our Baptism in its full significance is an act of consecration, by which every member of Christ is made one of a royal priesthood anointed by the Holy Spirit.

To describe all that is comprised in our Christian birthright, we should recite the several graces of the Holy Spirit by which He renews us in the likeness of our Lord and Saviour. Our birthright is the knowledge of our Father in Heaven as revealed in the Gospel of His Son : it is the pardon of our sins through the precious Blood of Christ; it is, besides, every virtue which belongs to sanctification : holiness, justice, truth, hope, love to God and to our neighbour. To be a partaker of the Spirit of Christ in all its fulness, to be heir to the glories of the Church triumphant, is a Christian's birthright. And it is this that we barter for pottage, if we yield to the temptation of the flesh and the world, by making temporal comfort the aim of our lives.

There is one aspect of life to which the idea of our adoptive birthright in Christ applies with special fitness. What is commonly called Honour in man or in woman, the honour of inviolate truth, of unblemished purity, belongs essentially to the privileges of our spiritual birthright : for it is not by nature, but by grace, that we have a right to claim that dignity which the idea of honour implies. Honour is not, as the world is apt to think, the prerogative of high birth, a virtue of the few, to which the many cannot aspire. It is a grace which invests every regenerate soul, without distinction of social degree. That chivalrous sentiment of honour which has added so much dignity to manhood and womanhood, is placed upon its true foundation when it is associated with the mystery of our adoption into the Communion of Saints. If a Christian sins he stains his honour; that is, he stains the purity of a soul redeemed by Christ and sanctified by the Holy Ghost, Who dwells in our bodies as in a temple. The sense of honour, which often degenerates into mere aristocratic pride, is exalted to a holy self-respect if we value our birthright as children of God, and feel the obligations imposed by a nobility so high.

From this point of view, Esau's example appears to touch us closely. All base ambition, or dissolute pleasure, all bartering of the goods of the spirit for the goods of the flesh, whether it be in public life, or in marriage, or in business, repeats the sin of Esau. And for us, as for him, there is a blessing associated with the birthright, yet distinct from it. Our blessing is life eternal, a life of which it is only one attribute to say that it endures for ever, seeing that not only in duration, but in all respects, life eternal is a glorified state beyond our present imagination.

To each of us there arise occasions when Satan tempts us to ask ourselves, "What profit shall this birthright do me?" In hours of weakness and depression we see the means of relief which can be had at once, though only on disgraceful conditions. Then let us call to mind the answer of our Lord to the tempter, " Man shall not live by bread alone, but by every word that proceedeth out of the mouth of God." Let us remember that our true life is not so much that of the body, which is mortal; but that of the soul, which is nourished and sustained by the breath of God. In our day, as of old, an evil spirit is at large upon the earth, tempting us to doubt the reality of things unseen: the spirit of negation, which mocks at all which cannot be seen, or touched, or tasted. Do not, brethren, listen to his subtle persuasion. Do not quench that spiritual light within, which reveals what eye hath not seen nor ear heard.

In the refectory of a Spanish convent there is a famous picture of the Lord's Supper, opposite to which an old man used to sit daily at his meals for fifty years: and as he reflected on the changes which had taken place among his brethren, how many had come, how many had passed away, while the silent figures on the wall remained, he said, " I am inclined to think that we, and not they, are the shadows."[1] Similar

[1] See Wordsworth's Poems, iv. 252.

to this is the conclusion forced upon us, when we meditate upon the ideas of Honour and Virtue, Truth and Holiness. They are forms of the mind, figures which group themselves in heavenly communion round the central figure of the Lord Jesus Christ. The profane may call them shadows. But generation after generation passes: we come and go, and they remain the same. Man's frame dissolves into dust, but Holiness and Truth continue what they were, for they are eternal. Their spiritual essence is more real than our bodies of flesh and blood. We, and not they, are the shadows.

VI. JACOB.

"Thy name shall be called no more Jacob, but Israel; for as a prince hast thou power with God and with men, and hast prevailed."—*Genesis* xxxii. 28.

(𝔖econd 𝔖unday in 𝔏ent, P.M.)

JACOB'S life is one of the most instructive in Holy Scripture. A life full of faults, yet distinguished above the lives of ordinary men by a rare force, intensity, and in some respects elevation of character, it is well worthy of our careful study, both for its many touches of human nature, and for an illustration of the Divine law, "Whom the Lord loveth He chasteneth; and scourgeth every son whom He receiveth." That which Jacob himself called his pilgrimage was a journey along a path chequered by light and shade, like his own character. The two names which he bore set forth the baser and nobler qualities which mingled in his nature. Jacob, or "supplanter," denotes that more than Eastern cunning by which he overreached in turn his brother, his father, his uncle Laban. The other name, Israel, or "a prince of God," denotes the strength of spiritual life, the earnestness of faith, and hope, and love, which makes his example memorable for all time. The name Jacob has remained a name for himself; the name Israel has been honoured above those of Abraham and Isaac as the enduring name of the Jewish nation; and not of them only, but, in a mystical sense, of the Church of Christ.

Much of Jacob's history seems to be recorded on purpose to teach the retributive justice of God. As he had sinned through covetous eagerness to possess his father's pastures and flocks and herds, and dependents, he was sent away into a distant land alone, to serve a harsh master for twenty-one years, suffering from heat by day and from frost by night, while he kept sleepless watch. As he had sinned through deceit, deceit was practised upon him. Leah was substituted for her sister Rachel, as he had passed himself for his brother Esau. Again, as he had dealt falsely with his father, so his own sons dealt falsely with him. That coat of Joseph's, stained with a kid's blood, was a deception which corresponded to his own, when he also slew a kid, to counterfeit Esau, and beguile his aged father. Nor was Rebekah's punishment less appropriate. She lost for the remainder of her life the presence of the home-keeping, affectionate son for whose sake she had deceived her husband. She never saw him again; but passed her last years in grief of mind, vexed by the wild moods of Esau, and by the alien women whom he took to wife.

Yet the blessing remained with Jacob. For God is merciful as well as just. He punishes, but He does not punish with the spitefulness of a vindictive man or woman, whose thirst of vengeance cannot be slaked. God's punishment is a fatherly correction, inflicted not for mere pain, but for discipline. He punished Jacob severely, very severely; but He did not hide His face from him.

And, if we look to the nobler side of Jacob's character, we can see that God had made him qualified for blessings which would have been thrown away on Esau's coarser nature. That far-reaching hope, which made him aspire to the birthright which Esau despised, shows a depth of soul beyond that of his brother. His patient labour for Rachel's sake is another sign of the strong hold which the unseen future had upon his mind, compared with the visible present.

A still more admirable feature in his character is that tender affectionateness of heart, of which there are so many instances throughout his life. His love for Rachel stands out in the Bible as one of the earliest and most beautiful examples of that conjugal affection which is the chief bond of human society. His fourteen years of servitude for her sake seemed a few days to him for the love that he bore to her. She alone was the wife of his choice; and his attachment to her is proved after her death, by his lasting preference of her children, Joseph and Benjamin, above all the rest. His tender care of Benjamin in his old age is an example of fatherly affection not less remarkable. We have learned from the lips of Jacob some of the most touching words in which an old man's love can be expressed, as when he says of Benjamin: "If mischief befall him by the way in the which ye go, then shall ye bring down my gray hairs with sorrow to the grave."

In harmony with this aspiring, patient, loving nature is the wonderful record of his angelic visions. His solitary journey from home to Padan-aram was cheered by that vision of angels ascending and descending which he saw at Bethel; and angels appeared to him afterwards at several of the decisive moments of his life, particularly when his exile came to an end, and he returned to the land which God had promised to give to him and his posterity.

When we read of Jacob's frequent communications with the spirit world, we have a key to the deeper secrets of his character. Visions are for those who have the spiritual sight by which alone they can be discerned. "The natural man receiveth not the things of the spirit of God." There are, indeed, some revelations which are manifest to the natural sense of every man, such as the thunders and lightnings which accompanied the giving of the law on Mount Sinai, and the dazzling aspect of the angel who terrified the soldiers at the Holy Sepulchre. But there is a nearer and more familiar perception of spiritual things, and of spiritual beings, which requires a corresponding faculty. When a voice from heaven answered the prayer of Christ, "Father, glorify thy name," some said "It thundered," others said, "An angel spake to him." When St. Paul heard Jesus speaking to him from heaven, his companions heard a sound also, but caught no articulate words.

There is a harmonious fitness in God's messages, answering to the nature of those to whom they are addressed. Spiritual messages delivered to a spiritual mind enter freely, and dwell there, but for others they are as books to one who cannot read.

Jacob was marked out before his birth, by that original fiat of God's will which forms the constitution of each one of us, as capable of a higher life than Esau; and through all his many trials, and many misdoings, he was not unfaithful to his high calling. That vision of Bethel inspired him with an abiding consciousness that the God of his fathers was with him. Again and again in his exile does he refer to this assurance as his help in trouble, when he had no friend on earth to help him.

An angel directed Jacob to return to the land of his kindred, and a company of angels greeted him on his arrival at Mahanaim. He was then about to encounter the danger that had caused his flight from home. Esau was not far off; and Jacob trembled with fear for himself and for the lives which were dear to him, his children and their mothers. A mind, so anxious and prudent as his, forms vivid pictures of possible evil. Every precaution is taken. He sends a message to his brother, entreating that he may "find grace in his sight," with a present carefully disposed so as to gratify his eyes and make him favourably inclined. He divides his family into two bands, that at least one may escape if Esau should attack either. Having done this, and led them over the ford of the river, he remains behind alone for the night (xxxii. 9).

There, in darkness and solitude, Jacob underwent a mysterious agony. In the words of the Prophet Hosea (xii. 4), "He had power with the angel and prevailed; he wept and made supplication unto him." He called to mind God's past mercies, and confessed his own unworthiness: he also called to mind God's promises, and prayed to be delivered from the hand of his brother. An angel appeared to him in the form of a man, with whom he wrestled all night, until the morning; and when the stranger bade him to let him go, he said, "I will not let thee go, except thou bless me." There it was that he won his name Israel, with the Divine assurance that he had prevailed with God.

To interpret in a literal sense this night-long wrestling of Jacob is as difficult as to interpret that ecstasy of St. Paul of which he himself said, "whether in the body, or out of the body, I cannot tell." There is this further parallel between the two, that they both were followed by a visitation of bodily infirmity, a "thorn in the flesh" in St. Paul's case, lameness in that of Jacob.

But the spiritual significance of this conflict is one upon which Christians have loved to dwell in all ages. Jacob wrestling with the angel is a symbol of earnest and effectual prayer, of prayer like that of which we read in the story of the Canaanite mother, the prayer which extorted from Christ the apparently reluctant blessing, "O woman, great is thy faith: be it unto thee even as thou wilt."

It is no play of fancy, brethren, but a true spiritual discernment, which has led so many Christian teachers and poets to see in Jacob wrestling with the angel an image of acceptable prayer. The lesson lies in the history itself, and the prophet Hosea has by Divine inspiration set the first example of drawing it out more clearly.

Rich and varied as is the instruction to be gained from Jacob's life, its spiritual lessons are concentrated in the two mysterious visits of angels which took place at his going out, and at his returning home: at Bethel and at Penuel. In both of these we read a message from God to man, which bears to be considered apart from its special reference to the patriarch Jacob, and applied individually to every human heart.

When we go forth from the home of our youth, to make experience of an unknown world, when the darkness finds us without a friend on earth, there is yet, if we have eyes to see it, a heavenly ladder set up from our resting-place, wherever it may be. We have in our Lord Jesus Christ a means of spiritual communication with the throne of God. Our prayers, winged by the Holy Spirit, go upwards: and the gracious gifts of the same Spirit come down to us, like ascending and descending angels. Thus the most barren, dreary, unfriended spot becomes through faith a Bethel, the "house of God" and the gate of heaven.

At the outset of the pilgrimage of life we need not desire anything more than this assurance of free communication with God in Christ. It is enough to know that we are not alone, but that the Lord Jesus, our Mediator and Advocate, is with us always, according to His promise, even to the end of the world. Nevertheless, it falls to our lot in the course of years to encounter, sooner or later, some great crisis, in which we feel a necessity for a renewed and closer sense of fellowship with the powers of the spiritual world. So even our Lord Himself, in His ministry on earth, underwent an agony in the Garden, before the sufferings of His trial and crucifixion. He, too, at the outset of His ministry had been comforted by the ministry of angels in the wilderness, and again at the close " there appeared an angel from heaven, strengthening Him."

Once at least in the life of each one of us, and possibly more than once, comes a crisis in which we are face to face with death, invested with all his terrors. It may be for our own sake that we are afraid: it may be for some life bound up with our own; a member of our own family, as dear or dearer than ourselves. Then, as we pray with confidence that God hears us, prayer becomes, if never so before, a real act of entreaty; not a form of words, not a religious solemnity, not a tribute of incense offered by our lips, but an actual struggle with the omnipotent power which encompasses us.

How to name that power we know not, in the agony of doubt and dread. The faith which moves along lightly in the sunshine of common life, is at fault in hours of extreme trial; as it were spreading out hands in the darkness, and ignorant what it catches hold of. "Tell me thy name," is the question that many a doubting heart asks of the unseen Power which sways its destiny. But only the strongest and noblest hearts have courage to say, "I will not let thee go, except thou bless me."

They are the true nation of Israel, the spiritual princes of God, who hold fast their faith in spite of the fears of human nature, grappling with adverse circumstances and extorting a blessing from what seems in the darkness to be an enemy, but whose

"Nature and whose name is Love."[1]

Such persistence in toil and in prayer is a sure note of the saints of God: as our Lord says, "The kingdom of heaven suffereth violence, and the violent take it by force."

Jacob, as we see him at the beginning of his life, is a remarkable instance of God's favour given without desert, as St. Paul particularly shows. "The children being not yet born, neither having done any good or evil, that the purpose of God according to election might stand, not of works, but of him that calleth, it was said unto her, The elder shall serve the

---

[1] See C. Wesley's Hymn, "Come, O thou Traveller unknown."

younger." Nevertheless, so far is God's favour to any man from smoothing his way of life, or absolving him from moral responsibility, that we find in this very example of Jacob the most notable illustration, perhaps, in all Scripture, of human will contending against adversity. The great patriarch, who gave his name to the chosen people of God, and has left on them the impress of his character, was not one whose path appeared strewn with flowers, and lighted by auspicious stars, but a much-labouring, much-sorrowing man, whose life was alternately a pilgrimage to a better country, and a wrestle against opposing fortune. God teaches us in him, that the chosen vessels of His grace are to be sought, not among those who take their portion in life most easily, but those who dare to say to the angel who threatens to crush them, "I will not let thee go, except thou bless me." For the love of God is hidden behind a veil from His most faithful servants, as it was above all when His dear Son gave His life for us, and died in pain upon the Cross.

VII. JOSEPH.

"The Lord blessed the Egyptian's house for Joseph's sake."—*Genesis* xxxix. 5.

(Third Sunday in Lent, P.M.)

HUMAN life is subject to general laws of God's providence, one of which is that which binds together the members of a family for good or evil, including even the servants of the house. The same cause which brings prosperity to one, brings prosperity in some measure to all. The same cause which brings adversity to one, brings adversity to all. These effects are sometimes easily explained; but often there are influences too subtle for human discernment, of which we can say only "This hath God done." As we read concerning Joseph, that the Lord blessed the Egyptian's house for his sake, and afterwards that his brethren were preserved through him, the blessing appears to be beyond the natural proportion of cause and effect, proceeding out of the overflowing abundance of God's bounty.

The working of God's law of fellowship comes in conflict with another of God's general laws, which brings to each reward or punishment according to individual desert. Moreover, there are far-reaching plans in the government of the world, which lead to the trial of acceptable men in the furnace of adversity. Thus we cannot account for the course of any man's life by one simple rule. Part of our lot in life we inherit, part is the consequence of our actions, part depends on providential circumstances of which we do not see the whole. Of this combined action of various influences we have a picture, whenever we watch the vessels at the mouth of a tidal river. There is the great body of fresh water from the river, flowing steadily down to the sea. There is the tide alternately ebbing and flowing. There is the wind, of which the sailors make a skilful use to save their labour: and there is, finally, the labour of the oarsmen, to be used when other means fail.

Joseph's history is a remarkable instance of the fluctuations of human life. His father's favourite, yet hated by his brothers: sold into exile, yet gaining the confidence of his foreign master: cast into prison, yet exalted to the prime ministry of the kingdom, he had full experience of the sweetness and bitterness of the world. But the most memorable fact in his history is that he became the saviour of his brethren, by the favour of God: and in this respect he has ever been regarded as a conspicuous type of our blessed Lord.

If we study Joseph's character we shall not fail to observe in him a spiritual grace, corresponding to the outward marks of God's favour. He was one of whom it can be said with truth that he "walked with God." Few men of whom we read have so distinctly realized to themselves the presence of God, as a righteous and merciful Lord. Alike in the sorrows of his youth and in the glory of his later years he bore in mind that the God of his fathers was with him, far away from his home and in the midst of the brilliant abominations of Egypt. His consciousness of God's presence was his safeguard under temptation, his comfort under affliction, and a restraining power to keep him from the sin of pride. It is in this respect that the example of Joseph stands out conspicuous, for the instruction of all who undergo similar trials. Tempted by Potiphar's wife he answers, "How can I do this great wickedness, and sin against God?" Bidden by Pharaoh to interpret his dream, he says, "It is not in me: God shall give Pharaoh an answer of peace." In making himself known to his brothers, he tells them, "It was not you that sent me hither, but God." These instances, to which others might be added, show the religious habit of his mind. A man cannot turn to God as he did, in the moment of sudden temptation, unless he is accustomed to think of God in the ordinary course of life.

Such loyalty to God is rare among us, though we have the advantages of Christian instruction, clearer and fuller than the simple knowledge which the Hebrew slave-boy carried into Egypt. I do not speak of those who dismiss the thought of God, and who believe or profess to believe that the world would go on as well without religion. Not only of these, but of those who bow themselves reverently in the house of God, there are not a few who forget His presence out of doors, especially when they are far from home and among strangers. Our ideas of God are apt to be so closely connected with the religious and social institutions under which we have been trained, that they fade away under new conditions. Duty is too often separated from worship, and considered merely as a formal rule, a law imposed by human society upon its members, without reference to God. Hence it often follows that in great cities and in foreign lands, where the fear of the world's judgment is taken away, those who live by a conventional standard of duty go astray, and only they who base their moral conduct on religious principles are fit to stand the trial. It is in this manner that all social duties are set before us in the New Testament. Parents and children, husbands and wives, masters and servants, are exhorted to fulfil their respective duties to each other, as to Christ.

Joseph's example is applicable to every condition: but the condition of a servant is the one to which it applies most closely and instructively. He had experience of every kind of servitude; from the thraldom of abject slavery to the responsibilities of a high ministry of state. In each position God prospered him, and his masters also because of him, according to the Psalmist's description of the way of a righteous man, "Look, whatsoever he doeth, it shall prosper." We shall not be wrong in attributing the prosperity of Joseph in great measure to such means as are within the reach of anyone: to diligence, prudence, and stainless integrity. Although it was a miraculous gift which first commended him to Pharaoh's notice, it was by the qualities of a good servant that he justified the confidence which Pharaoh placed in him. We can find many instances among the heroes of our Indian empire of men who have risen to eminence as Joseph rose, by faithful service; through God's favour, though without the aid of supernatural gifts; and there are some of these who have left an example, not only of temporal success, but of holy living. If at this day the millions of India enjoy a measure of peace and prosperity unknown under former dynasties, the effect is due mainly to God's blessing on the work of such men.

Success in life depends more than is commonly supposed on such simple virtues as truth and uprightness, industry and thrift, and less on extraordinary genius or rare opportunities. For those who have taken no pains to qualify themselves for useful service, it is impossible to say how many opportunities of usefulness slip away unobserved. The improvident and indolent and untrustworthy often wonder at the "good luck," as they call it, of a companion who prospers where they fail. In fact, however, similar "good luck" has offered itself to them, and they have not been ready. But the success in life, which is vaunted in biographies of "self-made" men is not the whole of the matter. What the world calls success is measured by station and riches; by titles of honour and a sumptuous household. There remain two questions to be asked concerning a successful man : What is his life in his own eyes? and, What is his life in the eyes of God? The magnificence which dazzles the world cannot stay God's judgment, nor even prevent that anticipation of judgment which a man's own conscience pronounces. Supposing that Joseph, in the plenitude of his power in Egypt, had hardened his heart against his own family, he would have been successful to little purpose in the end. Who would care to be a self-made Dives, meeting after death a Lazarus of his own kindred whom he had forgotten to relieve?

In the qualities for which Joseph is most praiseworthy, it is possible for the weakest and humblest to follow his example. The service which is rendered to an exacting invalid for Christ's sake, by a poor attendant, has often no recognition on earth, but stands recorded in the Book of Life. Watching and fasting and waiting upon a hundred capricious humours, the friendless drudge is harassed by continual reproaches, until it becomes a habit to find fault with whatever she does. But Christ is a friend to the friendless. He observes with love that never sleeps the hours of watching which receive no human thanks: and sometimes He blesses with unmerited benefits the patient, for the sake of the nurse who has his welfare at heart.

The subject before us suggests many serious reflections on the relation of master and servant. On both sides it is a relation of solemn responsibility. Masters and mistresses have in their hands an authority which in many cases is the very making of their servants' character. It is well known how a large household, or a large factory or business establishment, sets its mark upon the younger members for good or bad. To have been there is of itself a ground of praise or discredit. The house has what we call a tone, and for this the head of the house must be mainly responsible. When simple youths and maidens go from a cottage into domestic service, they must have more than ordinary strength of principle not to be moulded afresh by the ideas which they learn in the new society into which they enter. They must needs look up to their seniors for instruction in their work; and it follows naturally that they take their example altogether to be imitated. While the younger servants look to the elder, the elder look to the head, and thus the master of the house exercises an influence over many to whom he hardly speaks a word. The daily use of Family Prayer is a symbol and bond of Christian fellowship, when it is a real and not a formal act of united worship. But in order that it may be real, and may be felt to be real, there must be in the daily round of life such a habit of sympathy as Family Prayer implies.

Much depends on the choice of servants, whether a good character be valued as indispensable, or whether it be thought enough that a servant be useful as "a hand," fulfilling the particular work that is wanted. Especially is this the case with those servants who have the charge of their masters' children. Lessons which are taught in the nursery by word of mouth, or by example, leave a life-long impression behind them. Deceitful or uncleanly habits, and superstitious fears, learned in childhood, are not easily unlearned.

Among many faults in the choice of servants there is one which is condemned far less than it deserves, for the subject is one on which we shrink from speaking. I refer to the culpable folly of giving a mother's tenderest duty and privilege to a nurse whose qualification is her shame. They who consent to this cannot have reflected how they are accessory to a four-fold evil: tainting the blood of their own offspring in its source, sapping the morals of the household, corrupting far and wide the conscience of the poor, and closing up the springs of repentance and often of natural feeling in the poor nurse's heart, by making her sin profitable. If there is joy in heaven over a sinner that repents, if there is blessing on those who turn a sinner from error and save a soul from death, it can be no light matter to do the reverse of this, by sinking still deeper a soul which has fallen.

While in these and other respects a great responsibility lies on those who are at the head of a household, the servants also, from the least to the greatest, have their share in the duties on which the well-being of the whole family depends. Those who are engaged in domestic service have it for their main work in life. It is not as in a trade or profession, where a man's care is divided between his business and his family. A servant's business is, for the time being, the welfare of the family in which he or she is a member. Whatever account they have to render to God of their lives, must be in a great measure an account of their acts of service: whether they have been faithful to their trust, whether they have done their work as in God's sight, not with that which St. Paul calls "eye-service," the performance of duties only so far as it is likely to be seen. To act as in God's sight is the simple rule which solves many difficult questions, and it is the rule which the example of Joseph especially commends to us.

His character is one of the most perfect in Holy Scripture: a character in which tender affection is combined with far-sighted wisdom and unswerving sense of right. As to two points his conduct is open to question; but on each there is much to be said in his vindication. His father's partiality shown by his dress of many colours, and God's favour shown by his visions of future greatness, provoked the envy of his brothers. And it may easily have been that he was elated, as was not unnatural, at the favour shown to him by God and his father. If it were so, he was severely chastened by the discipline of sorrow. Again, when he brought to Jacob an evil report of his brothers, he appears at first sight to have acted too much as a spoiled child might act in telling tales. But there is a duty of loyalty to parents which overrules the general rule of hiding a brother's fault. And so, between masters and servants, there are occasions when the master's interest is so deeply at stake, that a servant who knows of evil doing and does not report it, becomes an accomplice in guilt. That which makes the character of a tale-bearer odious, is the seeking to win favour at the cost of a brother's or comrade's reputation. But this reproach must be incurred when the alternative is treachery to the head of the house. To think otherwise is the morality of brigands and conspirators, not of upright men. On the whole Joseph sets a noble example in this difficult matter. He was loyal as to his father's wrongs, generous and forgiving as to his own.

Finally, brethren, whether masters or servants, remember the obligation in which we all stand to Christ, as fellow-citizens of His Heavenly Kingdom. This world and its conditions will pass away. Differences of rank and fortune and station will be laid aside in the grave. But the virtues of faith in God's unseen presence, of hope in His gracious protection, of love to our Heavenly Father and our brethren, will abide. They descend from Heaven out of the fulness of the Holy Spirit, and they will bear, like the tree of life, all manner of fruit, both here and for eternity.

VIII. MOSES.

"God said unto Moses, *I AM THAT I AM:* and he said, Thus shalt thou say unto the children of Israel, *I AM* hath sent me unto you."—*Exodus* iii. 14.

(𝔉𝔦𝔣𝔱𝔥 𝔖𝔲𝔫𝔡𝔞𝔶 𝔦𝔫 𝔏𝔢𝔫𝔱, A.M.)

IN the whole Bible there is hardly to be found a weightier sentence than this, for it is the revelation of God to His chosen people by His most significant name. "I am that I am" is the English version of the Hebrew words which correspond to the name Jehovah. Thus the text is a message to all mankind that the God of Abraham, Isaac, and Jacob is not only the God of a family or tribe, but the True God, the Eternal. Upon this verse, with its context, is founded the mission of Moses to deliver his brethren, and the Covenant of Mount Sinai. Our Lord Jesus Christ refers to the same revelation, in close connection with two chief doctrines of the New Covenant—His own eternal Being and the Resurrection of the Dead. We have, therefore, abundant cause to meditate on it reverently. If it appear difficult at first sight, we shall not find it the less instructive and encouraging, when we study it carefully with the guidance of the Holy Spirit.

A few words are enough to recall the very interesting circumstances under which God spoke to Moses. The children of Israel were in bondage under the taskmasters of Egypt. Since the events of which we read last Sunday another Pharaoh had arisen who "knew not Joseph." A revolution, of which there are sundry records in the monuments of the land, deposed the line of shepherd kings, who were friendly to the Hebrews, and restored a native line, by whom they were bitterly hated. Moses had been educated as an Egyptian prince, but he chose to take part with his suffering brethren against their oppressors. He had to fly for his life; and in his exile he took refuge with a family of Abraham's race, and kept sheep in the pastures of Mount Horeb. Here it was that he was called by name, from the midst of a Bush which burned mysteriously without consuming, and warned that he was in the presence of the God of his fathers. The Voice foretold the redemption of the children of Israel from bondage, and the inheritance of the land of Canaan. Such was the fulfilment of the message to Moses, according to the letter. But its spirit belongs to all time.

God's revelation of Himself to Moses by the name Jehovah, or Eternal, was the planting of a faith which should endure for ever, and grow till it should embrace all nations in its perfected form. Our faith in Christ is rooted in this earlier revelation. For Christ reigns by the title of "Son of God," and this very title "Son of God" draws all its majesty from the sacredness with which God's holy name is invested. "Son of God" to heathen ears, has no such religious importance as to us. It means only the son of any of their numerous deities. That which makes the name so sacred to us is the association by which it is hallowed in Holy Scripture, which teaches us to worship only one God, the Almighty and Eternal. He was made known to Abraham as the Almighty; and His Name Jehovah is often used in the days of the patriarchs. But it acquired a new and most important significance in contrast to the religion of Egypt, and in relation to the founding of the commonwealth of Israel.

Even the visible sign of the Bush burning

with fire conveyed a spiritual truth. It was doubtless intended as a symbol of heavenly power coming down to earth, and that not to destroy but to preserve. The Jewish nation has been compared to the Burning Bush, as being marvellously kept alive through a fiery ordeal. I prefer, however, to regard the Burning Bush as a type of the sacred Branch of the stem of Jesse, whose human nature was penetrated through and through by the fire of His Divine nature.

But the enduring interest of the vision centres on the Name, " I am that I am ;" a name which later Jews refrained from uttering, so awful and majestic did it sound to them. Its meaning is embodied in the ascription of praise which St. John heard in heaven, when God is worshipped as He "which was, and which is, and which is to come." In other words, " I am that I am " signifies the Eternal, to whom Past and Future are as the Present, a Being not subject to the lapse of time. Accordingly, when the Lord Jesus said to the Jews, "Before Abraham was, I am," He was rightly understood by them to claim the essential attribute of God, Eternity. He who says " I am " in such a case assumes to himself the Divine nature. His words imply that which is declared concerning Christ in the Epistle to the Hebrews, that He is "the same yesterday, to-day, and for ever."

Many lessons, some of them spiritual, others practical, are suggested to us by the consideration of this great Name. For ourselves, to whom it is a necessary condition of life to mark the course of time by three divisions—Past, Present, and Future—it is vitally important to remember that in the Being of God all three divisions of time, Past, Present, Future, are gathered up into one everlasting Now.

1. God is the God of the Past. Therefore we receive the Holy Scriptures as "written for our learning," although they relate the dealings of God with races of men who lived on earth several thousand years ago. The Almighty, Who made the heavens and earth by His word, Who gave the first command of obedience to Adam and Eve, is the same God as He to Whom we kneel in prayer this day. The promises, the commands, the examples, the judgments, which stand recorded of the days of old, are applicable to our own case, for the God of the Past is our God. Nothing that has ever been is without some significance as an illustration of the laws of the Lord Jehovah. The New Covenant has made the first

old, but the God of the Old Covenant is the same as the God of the New, though manifested less completely. There is a gradual unfolding in Revelation of the Being and attributes of God. Revelation is properly the drawing back of the veil which hides God from us; but the veil is not drawn back all at once. Many a fold intervenes between us and the vision of God as He is. To some extent the veil was removed by Moses and the Prophets, and more by Christ and the Apostles. Yet the same eternal Trinity in Unity, the Father, Son, and Holy Ghost, abides for ever from the beginning.

2. Important as it is to recognize the truth that God is the God of the Past, manifested in Nature and in History, it is perhaps even more important to believe in Him as God of the Present. He is often called in Scripture "the living God," and "the true God," to distinguish Him from heathen gods such as Baal, or Jupiter, or idols, which have no real existence as living persons. If we realize what is meant by a living God, the effect of our faith will be to see His Hand in the course of our daily lives, to an extent far beyond anything that words can express. We shall live in the spirit of the cxxxixth Psalm, "Thou art about my path and

about my bed, and spiest out all my ways." Further, if we are sensible of the importance of faith in a true God, we shall not let our wishes or our fancy prevail over truth in our religion. I am speaking of a great and very common danger. A large part of mankind are culpably indifferent to truth in their religious belief, caring only to find peace and comfort to their souls by any means. This error lies at the root of popular Romanism. Under the names of Saints, some of whom were holy men and women, others of doubtful character, the ignorant are taught to look for help in trouble to intercessors, whose power to help is imaginary. Doubtless some of the legends of the Saints are beautiful tales, and I am far from denying the value of beautiful tales, even though they be nothing more, to stir in our hearts the love of goodness. But our souls need a surer foundation of faith to rest on, than mere imagination can supply. The great question as to religious doctrine is not the question, Is it beautiful, peaceful, comforting? but, Is it true? And thus the simple word "I am" expresses the most profound of all differences between the true God, and whatever else is worshipped in the place of God.

3. The Lord Jehovah is likewise the God of the Future. We shall not cease to be in His Hand when we pass out of this world into the world to come. A light has been thrown on this mysterious subject, by the words of Christ Himself, uttered with reference to the message of God to Moses (St. Luke xx. 37): "That the dead are raised, even Moses shewed at the bush, when he calleth the Lord the God of Abraham, and the God of Isaac, and the God of Jacob. For he is not a God of the dead, but of the living: for all live unto him." It would be inconsistent with the title "I am that I am," signifying Eternity, if Abraham were to rise no more, and God were to be called "the God of Abraham." From the two names of God revealed at the Burning Bush, "God of Abraham, Isaac, and Jacob," and "I am that I am," there follows by implication the truth of the Resurrection of the Dead. Nothing could be more incongruous, more self-contradictory, than to describe the Eternal God by the names of men who had died, if there were no resurrection.

We might have expected to find more in the Old Testament concerning the Resurrection of the Dead. The slight and obscure notices of a life to come in the Old Testament are a remarkable contrast to the prominence which is given in the New Testament to the doctrine of the Resurrection through Christ.

This subject is discussed at length in a celebrated treatise of Bishop Warburton's, "the Divine Legation of Moses," and it is made more intelligible by our modern researches into the religion of Egypt. We need only go into a museum of Egyptian antiquities, and see the mummies, embalmed with infinite care, which have been preserved for two thousand years, to understand that resurrection of the body was a doctrine in which Moses had been trained in Pharaoh's house. That he did not teach it to his brethren is to be explained by the fact, that they were already familiar with the idea, in a form which deprived it of spiritual value; for it was associated in Egypt with a degrading idolatry, which it was needful for them to forget. Moses was taught by inspiration to declare to the children of Israel the truth which they most required—that is, the actual presence of God with them, as a Ruler and Guide.

In considering these three aspects of God, as God of the Past, the Present, and the Future, we must not let any one point of view exclude the rest. We must not so read the histories of the Bible, as to lose sight of the close connection between God's dealings with His chosen people, and the laws of righteousness by which we are ruled at this day. Nor must we so interpret what is revealed of the life to come, as to contradict what we know of God's dealings in the past and the present. We must not suppose either His justice or His mercy to cease with this life.

How deeply Moses felt the power of the revelation of God's eternity, we see by the Psalm which is ascribed to him, the xcth in the Book of Psalms. In the Bible version this Psalm is entitled "A prayer of Moses the man of God," and it has for its subject the comparison of God's eternity with the transitory life of man: "Lord, thou hast been our refuge from one generation to another." Man grows up and withers like the grass of the field, while to God a thousand years are as a watch in the night.

Charged with this great truth, Moses went in God's name to be a minister of deliverance to His people in their bondage. And it is the same truth, as the foundation of all Christian doctrine, that the ministers of Christ have to deliver to souls in spiritual slavery. We proclaim the eternal Jehovah,

"Our help in ages past,
Our hope for years to come."

Old as this truth is, and familiar to us from childhood, it is like the sea or the sky, of inexhaustible freshness and infinite depth. We can never realize it fully, so as to say we know it well enough, for it presents day by day new lessons for our meditation. The eternity of God is a support to our souls when we lose confidence in all earthly things. Health is perishable: wealth is perishable: the whole order of society, political and moral, is undergoing changes, which tend we know not whither: the religion of our fathers is attacked by many formidable enemies. We have reason to fear, both privately and publicly, that the stream of time will carry away many things which are precious to us. But we need not lose heart while we believe that the eternal God is our refuge, and that His everlasting arms uphold us.

IX. KORAH.

"Even to-morrow the Lord will shew who are his, and who is holy."—*Numbers* xvi. 5.

(*First Sunday after Easter*, A.M.)

KORAH'S revolt and its punishment form one of the most impressive chapters in the history of Israel. The particulars of the rebellion come home to us, as presenting a close parallel to many an incident of our own time: while the strange and terrible judgment which destroyed the rebels, exceeds in its horror even the plagues of Egypt. If we recognize the principle that Holy Scripture was written for our learning, we cannot but see in the condemnation of Korah and his company a warning for all time against wickedness like his.

Rebellion against God, in the person of His representative, stands condemned in the example of Korah. Rebellion against parents, against rulers and governors of every degree, and, above all, against the Mediator and High Priest of the New Covenant, our Lord Jesus

Christ, has God's sentence recorded against it in this awful instance of His wrath. So plain is this lesson, that nothing can be said, in general terms, to make it more impressive. But the practical application requires all the greater care and discrimination; like the handling of a sharp-edged tool, which cuts both ways, and is apt to wound those who touch it incautiously. To understand what is, and what is not, a parallel to the rebellion of Korah, we must trace it from the beginning.

Korah, Dathan, and Abiram are named as the chiefs of the conspiracy against Moses, and we learn something beyond their names from the fact of their descent. For Korah was a Levite, cousin to Moses and Aaron, and therefore very near to the dignity of the priesthood. Dathan and Abiram were descended from Reuben, Jacob's first-born, who was superseded at one time by Joseph, at another by Levi, at another by Judah, in the leadership of the children of Israel. It appears that the Levites of the house of Kohath, to which Korah belonged, were encamped near to the Reubenites, on the south side of the Tabernacle.[1] Thus they had faci-

---

[1] See Blunt, "Undesigned Coincidences."

lities of conspiring together undiscovered until they had gained to their party 250 "princes of the assembly." Common jealousy bound together men who had nothing else in common. There was the Levite leader, so near to the High Priesthood that only one family intervened; there was the Reubenite leader, fretting under the tribal curse, "Unstable as water, thou shalt not excel," and wishful to regain his headship over Levi and the rest; yet both raising the cry of equality, for the temporary purpose of overthrowing the authority which God had set over them. "Ye take too much upon you" is the complaint of Korah against Moses, "Ye take too much upon you, seeing all the congregation are holy, every one of them, and the Lord is among them. Wherefore then lift ye up yourselves against the people of the Lord?" It might be yesterday, instead of three thousand years ago, that this plea of equal rights was put forward. Liberty, equality, and fraternity, great and sacred names, are taken for watchwords by the ambitious in order to cloak their selfish aims, in modern England and modern Europe, as among the tents of Israel in the wilderness.

For the right understanding of the story it is important to observe how far the conduct of

Moses was clear of blame in this matter. God's judgment given in his favour, both here and in the previous murmuring of Aaron and Miriam (Numbers xii.), is enough to vindicate him. But there is a remarkable passage in the eleventh chapter, which shows more vividly how free from pride or personal arrogance was the administration of Moses. He was told that two men, Eldad and Medad, prophesied in the camp, and Joshua said, "My lord Moses, forbid them." And Moses answered, "Enviest thou for my sake? Would God that all the Lord's people were prophets, and that the Lord would put his spirit upon them!"

Comparing this incident with that of Korah, we see the magnanimous character of the great Lawgiver of Israel, and we also see the vital distinction between the gift of prophecy and the office of the priesthood. Prophecy is God's immediate gift, apart from any ordained or constituted ministry. As such we should acknowledge it where we meet with it, the response of our spirits bearing witness to the presence of God's Spirit. Any devout Christian can feel, for instance, in reading Bunyan's "Pilgrim's Progress," that here is a man who has the gift of prophecy or spiritual utterance, though he has received no formal commission, and though his words betray defective instruction in Christian doctrine. He is like the man of whom the disciples said to Christ, "We found one casting out devils in thy name, and we forbade him, because he followeth not with us." But Jesus said, "Forbid him not."

While the gifts of God, under the Old and the New Covenant, are thus bestowed beyond the limits of the organized constitution of His kingdom on earth, there is not the less an organized constitution which God has ordained, and which His Minister is bound to uphold. Moses, patient and meek as he was, saw in the confederacy of Korah, Dathan, and Abiram a rebellion against God's appointed order, and to God's sentence he appealed, with the results we know: "The earth opened her mouth, and swallowed them up, and their households, and all the men that appertained unto Korah, and their goods. So they and all that appertained to them went down alive into the pit; and the earth closed upon them, and they perished from among the assembly."

Under both Covenants alike we find a plan of government divinely instituted, with ministers duly ordained, and endowed with spiritual gifts.

In each case we see the same regular symmetry of organization; first the Head, the Mediator of the Covenant, being Moses under the Old, and Christ under the New Dispensation; then the Chief Ministers under the Head—that is, the Twelve Patriarchs or Chiefs of the tribes of Israel, and the Twelve Apostles of Christ: under these, again, the seventy elders whom Moses appointed, and the seventy disciples whom Christ appointed. In these particulars, which correspond so evidently with each other, we see a manifest sanction given to the principle of orderly government in the Church. The conclusion to which we are led on the whole by a careful study of the analogies of the Old Testament and the light which is shed upon them in the Gospels and Epistles of the New Testament, is to distinguish the case of Korah widely from that of Eldad and Medad; and therefore to show a liberal toleration for the Eldads and Medads of our day, but to maintain firmly the order of the Church against its adversaries.

We must not overlook the self-willed, ambitious spirit which prompted Korah's revolt, or we shall misapply its lessons. God does not here, or elsewhere, teach us unlimited passive obedience. Of all histories in the world, perhaps, Jewish history is the richest in examples of conscientious opposition to wrong-doing, on the part of men in authority.

A remarkable instance occurs in the wanderings of the children of Israel in the wilderness, a few weeks before this time. Aaron had committed a great sin. He had received gold from the people, and had made for them an idol with it. As he said with miserable evasiveness, "I cast it into the fire, and there came out this calf." Then Moses called on those who were on the Lord's side to consecrate themselves, by taking His part; and the Levites stood forward as avengers of God's injured majesty. On that day, therefore, Korah found favour with God, while Aaron himself stood by, ashamed.

Another instructive case occurs in the Acts of the Apostles. St. Paul was brought up for examination in the presence of the High Priest Ananias, who ordered the bystanders to smite him on the mouth. Thereupon Paul said, "God shall smite thee, thou whited wall: for sittest thou to judge me according to the law, and commandest me to be smitten, contrary to the law?" But when they said, "Revilest thou God's High Priest?" he excused himself, saying,

"I wist not, brethren, that it was the High Priest; for it is written, Thou shalt not speak evil of the ruler of thy people." He showed respect for authority, even in a bad man. Yet he did not cease to maintain his just cause against the unrighteous minister of God. So also, when the same High Priest laid hands on Peter and John, "being grieved that they taught the people, and preached through Jesus the resurrection of the dead," the Apostles answered, "Whether it be right in the sight of God to hearken unto you more than unto God, judge ye. For we cannot but speak of those things which we have seen and heard."

Again and again in the history of the Church, official authority has been found on one side, and the Spirit of God on the other. Athanasius in exile defended the doctrine of the eternal Trinity in Unity against a world in error. Luther stood forth alone to protest against the iniquity and moral corruption of the see of Rome. Examples might be accumulated, even to the present century, of men who have appealed against God's unworthy ministers to God Himself, and whose appeal has been justified by posterity, although for a time it seemed to be in vain. There are other cases of insubordination also which, although not to be approved, may fairly be ascribed to conscientious error of judgment. Error of judgment is a fault, but it differs in degree and in kind from the sin of Korah.

Our application of the lesson of Korah's destruction must be limited to acts of rebellion in which self-will predominates. Yet this limitation leaves a wide field. For selfishness and ambition have many cunning disguises. A man who is discontented with his position, and seeks advancement, soon finds a grievance ready to his hand, and persuades himself that he is a champion of a public cause. Korah's plea, that all men are equal, is one of the most effective levers by which an ambitious man raises himself above his fellows. Perhaps he is only half aware what he is doing, and never sees himself as others see him. It is not only in great affairs that this ambitious spirit is manifested. Every station in life has its temptations, from the youngest member of a family to the highest rulers in Church and State. For illustration I will refer to three cases. There is the duty owed by children to their parents. There is the duty owed by members of the Church to their ministers. There is, thirdly, the duty owed by the clergy to Christ Himself as head of the Church. A few words on each of these three.

1. In a family, as the children grow up to manhood and womanhood, there is too often a rebellion against the authority of parents. Sons and daughters, flushed with self-esteem, forget their filial duty. They think scorn of the loving care which has brought them up, and the wisdom purchased by experience of which they know nothing. They will even impute to base motives the restraints put upon them for their own welfare. As when Korah accused Moses of wishing to put out the people's eyes and make himself a prince over them, so wilful children regard their parents as tyrannical governors, who want to hide the world from them, to keep them in subjection. It is a cause for guardian angels to weep over, when the rule of wise and loving parents is set at nought, and their hearts are broken at the sight of their rebellious children going to perdition. Although the earth opens not to swallow them suddenly, there is a spiritual fire from the Lord which comes forth sooner or later: the fire of remorse which may be quenched, and another fire, which may not be quenched.

2. As members of Christ's Church we have certain privileges and certain obligations. We read to-day in the Gospel, St. John xx., a solemn

commission given by Christ to the Apostles, "As my Father hath sent me, even so send I you." That commission was respected in the Church as the founding of a Christian society. It was not that the Apostles, or the clergy who succeeded them, had any special holiness. "The whole congregation are holy," as Korah truly said, although he drew from the saying a false inference, to support his rebellion. It is true that the Holy Spirit is given to every Christian soul for sanctification, and special gifts are bestowed at God's good pleasure on whomsoever He will, apart from the regular ministrations of the Church. But for the sake of order Christ has appointed offices which a man may not take to himself. Authority to administer God's Word and Sacraments, authority to pronounce forgiveness of sins in Christ's name, is not to be claimed by individual Christians as a right, but to be sought in dutiful obedience to the order of the Church Universal.

3. There is a further application of our subject which specially touches the clergy, inasmuch as we stand, like Korah, near to the sanctuary. Ambitious ministers, who intrude between Christ and His people, abusing their sacred office to gratify their love of power, are

followers of that guilty kinsman of Aaron of whom we have been reading to-day. Thus the boundless pretensions of the Roman Papacy are treason to the High Priest of the New Covenant; and the same ambitious spirit is not confined to Rome, but is manifested under Anglican surplices and Geneva gowns, whenever the ministers of Christ have thought more of being lords over God's heritage, than of being examples to the flock.

In all cases alike, the spirit which despises lawful government is contrary to God. Both as Christians and as citizens we are subject to the King of kings. The higher our privileges and the greater our liberty, the more we are bound to submit loyally to the authority of Him Who is higher than the highest, our Prophet-Priest, the Moses and the Aaron of the New Covenant, our Redeemer from Sin and Death, our Mediator at the Eternal Throne of Grace, our Leader to the promised land of Heaven.

X. BALAAM.

"Balaam the son of Bosor, who loved the wages of unrighteousness."—2 *Peter* ii. 15.

(Third Sunday after Easter.)

THE particular feature of Balaam's character which is noticed in the New Testament is his consent to do wrong for profit. He is described thus, not only by St. Peter, but by St. Jude; and while these lay stress on his love of riches, St. John in his Revelation refers to the evil which he did for that base motive. His sin is only too common, in all ages. But there is much in his history which makes his bad example stand out in singular distinctness and instructiveness. We have set before us in the Book of Numbers, almost as vividly as in a picture, the great Eastern prophet, as he stood on the cliffs of Moab, and surveyed the camp of Israel spread out in the valley below. He had been brought with difficulty from his home by the Euphrates, enticed by large promises of reward, that he might curse the invaders in the name of God. Such was the custom in ancient warfare. Before the armies went out to battle, their prophets or soothsayers [1] on either side invoked the blessing of the gods of their religion. Balaam was celebrated as being inspired with supernatural knowledge of the counsels of the Almighty. So the king of Moab spared no pains to obtain his assistance. He would not take Balaam's first refusal, but sent a second and more flattering message, which at first sight appeared to be successful, for it brought the prophet to his aid.

Seven altars are erected on the brow of the hill, and a bullock and a ram are prepared for sacrifice on each. Then the prophet goes from altar to altar, and offers the twofold sacrifice with due solemnity seven times. After this, he retires to a high place alone, to await the moment of inspiration. Balak and the chiefs of Moab look on, expecting the oracle anxiously. After a while the prophet returns as one in a trance, full of the message of God which he has received. We have to imagine him carried out of himself by spiritual rapture, his blood-stained hands

---

[1] See Smith's Dict. Antiquities, "Fetiales."

outspread over the windy precipice, his eyes glaring with an unearthly light, as he utters in a rhythmic chant the words which God has put into his mouth.

To the horror of the Moabite princes, his words are not a curse but a blessing upon their enemy. The king expostulates with him in vain. Balaam declares that he has no power to speak according to his own will. All the rewards of Balak could not move him to prophesy otherwise than as God inspired him. Another place is tried, and then a third; but at each remove the blessing is more emphatic. Whether his eyes ranged freely over the numberless hosts of Israel, or only caught sight of a portion between the clefts of the rocks, he could not choose but say, "This people is blessed."

We have a deep source of comfort, applicable to ourselves, in the fact of the blessing which Balaam was inspired to pronounce on Israel. For the children of Israel, as we read very fully in the Book of Numbers, were guilty of many transgressions against God's law at this time. Anyone who might have walked among their tents, using no prophetic insight, but natural observation, would have seen and heard much to reprove; the envy of the several tribes, the murmuring of the baser sort at the sameness of their life and their food; the ungovernable passions, the stiffness of neck, and hardness of heart, which from time to time provoked the wrath of God against His people. The particulars of their conduct seem for the most part to be a tissue of misdoing. Yet we see here that they are not rejected by God. On the contrary, they are declared to be a holy people. Thus we may hope that the spots and blemishes, which mark the Church of Christ throughout the details of its history, disappear when surveyed from heights above. The Israel of God, whether seen in full or partially, is blessed still as a whole, notwithstanding individual faults.

I believe it is right, brethren, to apply a judgment of the same kind to the society in which we live. Our minds are apt to be filled with the memory of evil doings, which is clearer and longer in most than the memory of what is done well. Thus we may easily pass too harsh a judgment, for "in many things we offend all." Our excess of severity will be restrained, if we look less at details, and more at characters as a whole, surveying our neighbours from a comprehensive point of view, like that on which

Balaam stood. So we shall see the pillar of the cloud of God's favour resting on some households, in which we have seen only faults and deficiencies while living amongst them. Charity often prompts this view of men when they die, but we ought not to wait for death to be just.

There is much besides in Balaam's prophecy which demands our careful study, especially its sublime and wonderful anticipation of the Messiah, the true Star and Sceptre of Israel. But the subject which claims our attention in these chapters of the Book of Numbers, as we read them consecutively, is the character of the prophet himself, one of the most interesting and remarkable in the Bible. Several of the best sermons in our language have been written to expound the character of Balaam. One (Bishop Butler's) has shown how strong was the sense of good and evil in him, though he did not act according to his conscience. Others (by Newman and Robertson) have shown how he fell by trifling with his conscience. For he is a signal example of that common inconsistency in human nature, which is described by St. Paul as a war between the law of our mind and a contrary law in our members. His conscience drew him one way, and his desires another.

It was against his own wish that he pronounced a blessing on Israel. He would have chosen to accept the presents of the King of Moab, and spoken in accordance with the King's request. In spite of God's warning at first, forbidding him to go, he asked again; and the second time God bade him go, punishing him, as he often punishes wilful men, by consenting to his desire. So he went; and on the way he had a strange and mysterious rebuke from the ass he rode on, as if to teach him and us the lesson, that the dullest of brutes is wiser than a highly-gifted man who shuts his eyes to God's commands. When he met Balak, he endeavoured to prepare the king's mind for disappointment. He knew that the prophetic gift was no part of himself, that he must utter, not what he chose, but what God taught him to utter. The King of Moab could not understand this. He thought that the gift of God might be had for money, that Balaam's soul would yield to liberal offers; and thus he persisted, to his own confusion, in striving to obtain a curse upon his enemies by means of gifts.

Yet, although the Moabite King mistook the operation of the Spirit of God in Balaam, he had not mistaken his man. The prophet was willing enough to serve him by any means which lay in his own power. We read in a later chapter (chap. xxxi.) how Balaam actually suggested to the king insidious ways to defeat his own inspired blessing. By his advice the Moabites and Midianites conspired to bring a curse upon the children of Israel by tempting them to idolatry and sensual vices. He was, indeed, so far successful that the children of Israel were punished for their sin by a plague. Then the Moabites and Midianites hoped to overcome their reduced strength; but they were defeated, and the wicked prophet fell in the battle.

Our interest in Balaam turns mainly on the struggle in his nature between a Divine inspiration of righteousness, and a selfish will which was set on earthly objects. The contrast, as it is set forth in Holy Scripture, appears strange, even marvellous. Nevertheless, it is a type of character which is not without parallel. There have been great men in modern times who have been drawn in a similar manner by the opposing influences of a good and a bad spirit within them. One of the most famous of these has been described in the bitter verse:

"The wisest, brightest, meanest of mankind."

A man may speak as a prophet of God, may have his mind enlightened by a surpassing illumination, not of intellect only, but of spirit; he may be so far loyal to the Divine voice within him as to speak the truth; and yet his practical life may move altogether in another sphere, seeking base ends for himself. Many a writer, whose moving language touches the hearts of others with pure and holy emotion, is merely seeking gain. Actors, whose counterfeit passion melts an audience in tears, are often thoroughly mercenary themselves. Are there not also preachers, whose preaching is little else but acting? And thus—to come to the point which chiefly concerns us—our life, for every one of us, is divided into two parts, the sentimental and the practical: the first part a life of ideas and emotions, and in some sense visions: the second part a life of action, and of plans which lead to action. These two parts combine together in a well-ordered soul; but in souls which are ill-regulated, as Balaam's, they are at variance. The visions and ideas are heavenly; the actions and plans are earthly.

For those who are endowed with spiritual gifts in an extraordinary measure, there is sometimes, as with Balaam, a certain dignity of spiritual tone which is sustained in spite of moral baseness. A man so endowed is upheld in thought and speech by the force of conscience within him, so that he cannot be "disobedient to the heavenly vision" in word, however unworthy his actions may be. But such instances are rare. More commonly men, whose spiritual and moral life are out of harmony, sink into hypocrites. Their spirituality becomes a mere pretence, cloaking their avarice or ambition.

Now this is a real and terrible danger to which we are subject. Who is not aware how often men of devout and even saintly religious profession are found wanting in the virtues of ordinary life, in common honesty, sobriety, or truthfulness? It requires, unhappily, very little knowledge of mankind to bring to our notice cases of sanctimonious professions joined in the same person with unscrupulous worldliness of conduct. In such cases we are apt to think the man is acting a part. Yet he probably deceives himself more than anyone else. When he talks of himself as called by Providence to do what he is doing for gain, and would not do other wise, he is really believing what he says; but he has misused his gifts of spiritual discernment until he has become unable to recognise the intimations of God's will which are at variance with his own will.

There is a touching pathos in Balaam's aspiration, "Let me die the death of the righteous, and let my last end be like his!" Connecting this wish, which he uttered as he gazed on the tents of Israel, with his actual death soon afterwards in guilt and shame, we cannot but feel some touch of human sympathy, if we call to mind how little our best wishes have been fulfilled in our own subsequent conduct. How bitter is the pang of regret with which one who has seen and approved the good, but followed the evil, looks upon the course of another's well-spent life, which it is too late to copy! There are few indeed, however upright in their general conduct, however disposed to be satisfied with themselves, who will not feel conscience-stricken for some things done amiss, some chapters of their past life which mar the consistency of the whole, and which they would blot out if they could.

When we consider how Balaam, with all his gifts, has left a name of reproach behind him to later generations, we must also consider that every one of us is liable to a similar judgment if we follow his fault, loving the wages of unrighteousness. Not here, perhaps, for human praise and blame can only take account of a few conspicuous names. The memory of ordinary men, their righteousness or unrighteousness, fades quickly away from this world. By the time the grass has grown afresh upon their graves, there are only a few kindly hearts which cherish the remembrance of what they were. But in the book of God the past lives still, and the hidden transgressions of former years shall be brought to light when the dead rise again: when, as Daniel writes, they "That sleep in the dust of the earth shall awake, some to everlasting life, and some to shame and everlasting contempt."

Two voices call us, the voice of God speaking to us through the gospel of the Lord Jesus Christ, and the voice of Satan, speaking to us through the temptations of the world and the flesh. So long as we hold our hearts open willingly to receive God's spirit, we shall be able to distinguish the voice of God from that of the tempter. But the temptations of the world, and more particularly the love of money, are apt to dull the spiritual discernment of right and wrong, even in those who are most highly endowed. Unless we apply the truths which God has revealed to us to our daily conduct, we shall fall into inconsistencies like Balaam, his perception of truth at one time raised above humanity by spiritual knowledge, at another time sunk below that of a brute beast by self-willed blindness of heart. His history records the ruin of a noble soul. But there are also noble souls among us, precious in God's eyes, though unrecognised by man, trembling in the balance between good and evil. Pray for yourselves, and for each other, brethren, that you may have not only a clear knowledge of God's will, but also what is indispensable, a hearty desire and strength to do His will, according to the knowledge which He gives you.

XI. JOSHUA.

"As I was with Moses, so will I be with thee."
Joshua, iii. 7.

(𝔉irst 𝔖unday after 𝔗rinity, A.M.)

LIKE many of the greatest and best of men, Moses died with the work of his life unfinished. God refused to him that which would have rounded off his task, as leader of the children of Israel into the Promised Land. The book of Deuteronomy closes with his death on the other side of Jordan; and in the first verse of the following book we read how his servant, Joshua the son of Nun, was called to take his place as leader, and undertake the conquest of Canaan.

Joshua's commission was of a different kind from that of Moses. He was to act rather than to speak. Moses had been bidden to deliver God's law to the people. He had spread out his hands in intercessory prayer while the people fought with Amalek, and the fatal error of his life had been to strike an impatient blow, when he "spake unadvisedly with his lips." Joshua, on the contrary, was a man of action; a soldier, not a prophet. He was bidden to make war against seven powerful nations, whom the children of Israel regarded with not unreasonable dread as their superiors in bodily stature and in arts of every kind. God's charge to him, three times repeated, was "Be strong and of a good courage."

He was an instrument well fitted for the work to be done. Brave, prompt, patient, well-trained to obey or to command, Joshua is a pattern of soldierly virtues. Such a character must needs be respected in any age, whether we meet with it in friend or in enemy. The gentler graces of the spirit of Christ are never more fruitful than when they are sown in a nature like Joshua's. A man whose heart is full of religious devotion, whose courage is developed and restrained by habits of military discipline, will take a prominent place in the army of Christ, when he has once enlisted under Christ's banner. We have an example of the kind in the centurion Cornelius, and many of us can call to mind others in the course of our reading, or, it may be, in our experience.

When the chief command was given to Joshua,

he was subjected to a trial which was characteristic of the peculiar training of the Hebrew nation. He was taught in various ways that he was no more than God's lieutenant. First, he was given to understand, by a mysterious vision, that the true Captain of the Lord's Host was Another, to whom he must show reverence, taking his shoes from off his feet. Then Jericho fell, not by human valour, nor by strategy, but by faith in God's word. Day after day the army marched round the walls in a religious procession, headed by the priests and the Ark. At last, on the seventh day, when they had completed the circuit seven times, they raised the war-shout: and thereupon the walls fell down miraculously, and the children of Israel took possession with ease of the panic-stricken city.

The strict obligation of obedience, which God imposed on his chosen people, was illustrated immediately after the taking of Jericho by the case of Achan. His act of covetousness, in reserving a part of the accursed spoil, brought defeat on the host; and victory returned to them only when the offender had been detected and put to death.

Another Divine law, which Joshua observed strictly, was faithfulness to his plighted word.

He kept faith with Rahab, and protected her house in the destruction of Jericho. He also kept faith with the deceitful Gibeonites, and fought for them against the confederate kings of Canaan.

The great battle of Gibeon is the turning point of Joshua's history, both in its natural and supernatural incidents. A plain narrative of the facts would run thus: Gibeon was attacked by five kings, or chiefs, and Joshua marched during the night, twenty or more English miles, to fall upon the confederate army by surprise at daybreak. First up the hill, then over the pass and down the western valley of Ajalon, the host of Israel drove the heathen before them, and a tremendous hailstorm, which broke upon the flying Canaanites, completed their defeat.

To these facts, memorable enough in themselves, a wonderful addition is made by the inspired writer of the Book of Joshua, quoting from a more ancient poetical book, the Book of Jasher, in which the Sun and Moon are described as standing still at Joshua's command. I do not think we are called upon to understand this famous passage literally; for some of the best Jewish scholars, centuries before the difficulties of modern astronomy were raised, interpreted the standing still of the Sun and Moon as a poetical image, like many which we find in the Psalms and the Prophets.[1] Yet there is undoubtedly more in the description than what we commonly mean by poetical imagery; for the words of Scripture suggest the idea that the Sun and Moon, the gods of the Canaanites, were on that day shown to be unable to defend their worshippers against the God of Israel. Baal the Sun-god, Astarte the Queen of Heaven, shone down alternately on the host of Israel, and lighted them to victory, as if obedient to the will of Joshua. The full moon, which guided him upon his difficult path from the Jordan valley to the mountain heights of Gibeon, and on the following night enabled him to track the five kings to their hiding place, appeared to join with the sun in service to the soldiers of the Lord Jehovah.

The victory gained by Joshua was not merely a victory of one people over another people, but of one religion over another: and this is the chief significance of the record in Holy Scripture. Volumes have been written on this subject,

[1] See Keil, Joshua; and Speaker's Commentary, ii. 55.

without making it much clearer. What I have said will be sufficient to indicate the interpretation which seems most probable, of one of the most difficult passages in the Bible. In these days, when science is taken by some as a substitute for religion, and the laws of the physical universe are apt to be put in place of God, we have reason to fall back on the great lesson of Joshua's victory, that the Lord of all is not to be found in the phenomena of nature, but above them; not in the Sun or Moon, but in the Eternal Maker of the Sun and Moon.

Another serious question, hardly less important, is raised by the conclusion of the same chapter, in which we read Joshua's treatment of the defeated kings. They are dragged out of the cave in which they lay hidden, and put to a shameful death. Joshua's captains set their feet on their necks, and their corpses were hung up on trees as a final indignity.

Elsewhere, in our own English history, we have examples of a very different behaviour towards a fallen enemy. The English prince, who waited with his own hands on the king whom he had taken prisoner in battle, presents a singular contrast to the Jewish conqueror. The English king, who pardoned the archer who had given him his death-wound, is another notable instance of generosity to enemies. Nor is it only Christian chivalry which supplies such examples. We have similar touches of humanity in the Greek Alexander, protecting the family of his enemy Darius; and in the Roman Scipio, moved with sympathy at the fall of Carthage.

There can be no doubt whatever, that examples like these are much fitter for our imitation, than the fierce conduct of Joshua and his captains. Our difficulty is not to know how we ought to behave, for Christian education guides us practically; but how to reconcile to our Christian principles the fact, that Joshua, a holy man of old, acted thus. The question arises, not once or twice, but constantly throughout the Old Testament. The merciless cruelty towards enemies, of which Joshua's treatment of the defeated kings is an instance, does not stand out alone as a rare exception, but is the common rule in the wars of Israel. It is conspicuous in the acts of the men who are held up to admiration: as when Gideon put to death his Midianite prisoners in cold blood, or when Samuel hewed in pieces Agag the king of the Amalekites, or when David massacred his enemies on several occasions. On the other hand, Saul was reproved for sparing the king whom he had taken prisoner. And the laws of Moses lay down with the utmost rigour a command of exterminating warfare against the nations of Canaan: to "smite them, and utterly destroy them," to "make no covenant with them, nor shew mercy unto them."

Plainly, we must draw a broad distinction between the Spirit of the Old Covenant and that of the New. We must recognize an incompleteness, a narrowness, in the Old Dispensation, which we are thankful to have outgrown by the grace of the Spirit of Christ. "The law made nothing perfect." It was "a schoolmaster," or usher, "to bring us to Christ." So much is plain, but that is not all. To reconcile the Old Testament and the New, as parts of one Divine revelation, we must show that the life of Joshua has lessons of conduct for us, notwithstanding our utter abhorrence of the barbarities of Hebrew warfare.

What lessons those are, we can see by returning to the comparison which I drew just now, of the courtesies of Christian knighthood, as illustrated by the Black Prince and Richard Cœur de Lion. We miss in them the religious earnestness which moved the warriors of Israel.

Our English Edward and Richard fought for selfish glory, delighting in the exercise of their skill as horsemen and swordsmen. But Joshua, and men like him, went into battle with grave seriousness, as ministers of God to extirpate evil. His mission was to establish a holy nation, in the place of a wicked nation which was accursed by God. He had not attained to the spiritual discernment which separates a man and his actions, treating the man as a brother, and punishing his actions as they deserve, without hatred to him. To a blunt soldier like Joshua, mercy appears mere weakness, or else treason to the cause of righteousness.

It is easy to be gentle in a cause for which we do not care, but to combine gentleness with earnestness is a task which demands the highest religious and moral culture, a degree of culture to which the Israelites had not attained, and which is but rarely attained now, after centuries of Christian teaching.

Our modern history supplies a very remarkable parallel to that of Joshua, in the conquest of India. The land was like Canaan, flowing with milk and honey, and possessed by idolatrous nations, the cup of whose iniquity was full. A small number of invaders succeeded, by God's favour, in subduing the Kings of Hindostan, one after another; and the people found their gods powerless to defend them. So far the two cases resemble each other. In some other respects the difference is wide. Zeal for the one true God, which filled the soul of Joshua, has little place in the record of our Indian empire. Our rule has been marked by a spirit of toleration, not to say indifference, which left undisturbed the hideous idolatry of Juggernaut; and at this day Mussulman and Hindoo enjoy, alike with Christian, the protection of a mild and equitable government. There could not be a greater contrast than the religious neutrality of the conquerors of India, as against the intolerance of the conquerors of Canaan.

A few have been found, however, uniting as fervent a zeal for God as the heroes of Israel, with as tender and comprehensive a humanity as that which the Gospel of Christ teaches. Such men as the Lawrences, Havelock, and Edwardes, are true followers of the Joshua of the New Testament, Who came not to destroy men's lives, but to save them.

The parallel between our Lord Jesus Christ and Joshua, which is suggested by His bearing the same name, and illustrated by His work of leading His chosen people to a heavenly Land of Promise, throws light on the problem of reconciling love to God and love to man.

Our Saviour's life on earth was a warfare. He fought with the sword of the Spirit, which is the word of God, against falsehood, against pride, against selfishness, in short, against all the powers of evil in the world. The sun was darkened with preternatural gloom while He fought out the decisive battle of the Cross. Afterwards, when He ascended in triumph to His Father's right hand, He used His power, not to humble His enemies, but to give gifts to men, even for His enemies, that the Lord God might dwell among them.

His example shows us that zeal for God is compatible with charity to man. We may be earnest in God's cause, and yet gentle to our opponents. And this is a truth which comes home to the daily life of many of us. From time to time our duty compels us to act for God's sake, in opposition to some whom we honestly believe to be in the wrong. It is so in great questions of the Church or the State; it is so in lesser questions, as to the administration of a hospital, a school, or a household. In proportion as we are in earnest, our hearts go forth into the fray, and we are tempted to forget that our opponents are our brethren. At such times, let us ponder the lessons of mercy set before us by the Captain of our Salvation. Love victorious through suffering is the great lesson of the Cross: and that spiritual victory binds together the conquerors and the conquered in united thankfulness to God through Christ, in that City of God which has no need of Sun or Moon to lighten it, in the presence of His eternal glory.

XII. SAMSON.

"The child shall be a Nazarite unto God."
Judges xiii. 5.

IN these words the angel who appeared to Samson's mother described her unborn son. His message and miraculous appearance remind us of a far more memorable prediction in the New Testament, the annunciation of the birth of Christ, which was made to Mary by the angel Gabriel. Probably the likeness between these two heavenly messages was in the mind of St. Matthew, when he applied to the child Jesus the words, "He shall be called a Nazarene," as prophetic words fulfilled by His residence at Nazareth. It is true that the connection between the words "Nazarene" and "Nazarite" is only a close resemblance of sound; but the verbal likeness points to a deeper analogy between a type and its fulfilment. St. Matthew suggests, by this allusion to Samson, how the Saviour of the world was foreshadowed by the great Judge of Israel. The significance of Samson as a type of Christ is a subject which requires and deserves attentive consideration. What we call types in Holy Scripture are partial likenesses of Christ or of His kingdom, which hold good in some particulars, but not in all. Thus the Paschal Lamb represents Christ in His innocence and in His death, the Scape-goat represents Him in His bearing the sins of the people, the Brazen Serpent in being lifted up as a means of salvation through faith. God has been pleased to teach the world the elements of Divine truth after the manner in which children are sometimes taught their letters. A child is shown each letter by itself, with a picture alongside to help the memory. Such is the mode of teaching by types which is used in the Old Testament. Each several feature of the character of the Son of God is represented by some appropriate image, which serves as an illustration. Neither the Paschal Lamb, nor the Scape-goat, nor the Brazen Serpent is a complete type of Christ, but only in respect to certain of His attributes. So also the persons who are distinguished as types of Him, Abel the murdered shepherd, Isaac the child of promise, Moses the mediator of the Old Covenant, Solomon the prince of peace—these, and many more, are limited in their resemblance to some one portion of the manifold character of the Lord Jesus, in whom all prophecy was fulfilled.

We might hesitate at first sight to recognize in Samson a type of Christ; for his life presents to us little that is good, and as to his general character he stands in marked contrast to the pure holiness of the Son of God. It is only when we regard him as a great deliverer of Israel, conspicuous beyond all others during the lawless period of the Judges, that we find a clue to the spiritual interpretation of his history. Then we observe, further, that the circumstances with which God surrounded his life are in a high degree suggestive. His birth is one of the very few which were announced by an angel. He was specially dedicated to God as a Nazarite; and this vow of dedication was a symbol of holiness to be fulfilled, though in a different manner, by the true Saviour of Israel. Then, as Samson grew up to manhood, the gifts of God in him were shown by mighty works: the first of which is associated with a marriage-feast. A later work, still more significant, consisted in his bearing away the gates of the fortress in which he was imprisoned, a vivid image of Christ leading captivity captive by rising from the grave. Samson's betrayal by his friends, his being bound with cords which he could have broken if he would, are more or less typical; but most of all, his crowning victory in death, and by means of death. Resemblances like these are indications of the unity of plan which pervades God's eternal scheme of redemption. In the early Church they used to be magnified beyond their due measure, but they are now too little regarded.

Passing on from the incidents and circumstances of Samson's life, to consider his personal qualities, we find him distinguished in a supernatural degree by one gift which is highly valued by all mankind, the gift of strength. So much was his strength beyond the ordinary measure of human force, that it is ascribed as miraculous to the Spirit of the Lord; for instance, when he rent a young lion with his hands, when he broke the cords with which he was bound, and slew a thousand Philistines with the jaw-bone of an ass. On these occasions it is said that the Spirit of the Lord came upon him, and on the other hand we read that the Lord departed from him when he lost his strength by the treachery of Delilah. To this gift of bodily strength, he added another, for which he is commended in the Epistle to the Hebrews; namely a power of faith by which he "waxed valiant in fight and turned to flight the armies of the aliens." He did not, as do some highly-favoured men, mistrust God's favours. His daring was fully in proportion to his strength. He went forth into danger with a cheerful and confident valour, which showed that he put unhesitating faith in the Lord God of Israel.

Little more than this can be said in his praise. Of the nobler qualities of faith, the patience, the self-devotion, the humility, the purity, the hope and love, which spring from faith in its perfection, there are few traces, if any, in the life of Samson. And yet, taking him simply as he was, his character is instructive, both in its lights and shadows. We are reminded by Holy Scripture in his history that bodily strength is a gift, and a precious gift of God, who has made the qualities of force and courage to have a mighty influence in the world. We can see that it is so at this day. Not only the young, but grown men and women look with admiration on a man who is strong and brave. Of the prizes of boyhood few are more esteemed than those which are won in athletic sports; and no star of gold conveys greater distinction than the simple cross of bronze, which is awarded for valour on the battle field. So they who excel in feats of arms take a high place in popular estimation even yet; although modern times give more advantage to powers of the mind, to inventive skill, to forethought, to organization and government. The actual rulers and judges of nations are no longer warriors, fighting hand to hand, yet in a more limited sphere the gifts of a Samson are held in honour, and impose a high responsibility on any one who is endowed with them. Boys and young men often take for their ideal of excellence a hero like Samson.

But the possession of gifts from God is a cause of many temptations, and in this respect the life of Samson is full of warning. His great gifts were perverted to selfishness. When we look below the splendour of his wonderful career, to the heart of the man himself, we find there a ruling passion of self-indulgence. He made havoc of the Philistines, but it was mainly for his own sport. He had no serious loyalty to his nation or to God. His mighty works were done for revenge, or for wanton mischief. There was in him none of the earnestness of Joshua or of Gideon, but a levity of character, which not unfrequently accompanies great bodily strength. Milton, in his sympathy with Samson's blindness and affliction, has invested him with attributes which do not belong to his character, as represented in the Bible. He was a light-hearted athlete, fond of jests, which were often destructive and cruel. One of his faults was that which is condemned in Scripture as the very root of sin. He loved strange women. This is named throughout the Bible, along with idolatry, as the two great evils, which beset the soul of man. Again and again the union of Christ and His Church is compared to the holy bond of marriage, and unhallowed love is the symbol of the mystery of iniquity. There is a divinely ordained connection between pure morality and pure faith. License in belief and licentiousness in practice are apt to go hand in hand, for both alike spring from a rebellion of man's will against the will of God.

The gifts which God bestowed on Samson were spent in wilful caprice, to gratify his selfish humour, his lust, or his revenge. Even at the last, when calamity might have chastened his soul, when in his blindness he clasped the pillars of Dagon's temple, and raised his sightless orbs in prayer, his petition was a selfish one. He asked to be strengthened only this once, that he may be avenged of the Philistines for his two eyes. No high thought, such as moved the youthful David when he went out against the giant, or Gideon when he refused the kingdom, stirred the soul of Samson. He died as he had lived.

Nevertheless, this great champion is a fair example of a large class of the world's heroes. Regarded in the pure daylight of the Bible, he appears an image of base metal, partly of iron and partly of clay: but in the false glare of vulgar history he seems heroic. No knight of romance was more daring than he, when he suffered his enemies to tie his hands, secure in his incomparable strength; or when he invaded their city alone, in search of adventures. If, as the world has sometimes thought, revenge is a manly virtue, who more triumphant in revenge than he? Or if lawless love, as some professed Christians are not ashamed to think, be consistent with an ideal of manliness, it was for this that Samson wasted his divine gifts, and closed his days in miserable darkness. Not only in heathendon but in Christendom these qualities have often been admired, especially when set off, as in Samson, by a gay and festive temper. Many captains and kings of high renown have run a course resembling his, less in his gifts than in his vices. Chivalry has its Nazarites, spotless in conventional honour according to their own law, but dead to a sense of purity or compassion. Others however might be named, who have shone in arms with a fame as brilliant as that of the bravest, and have preserved an unsullied reputation by God's grace. There is, for instance, that devout hero of the Middle Ages, Godfrey, the leader of the first Crusade. There is Bayard, and our own Sidney.

But the valour which is characteristic of Christ's followers is distinguished by force which is not the less mighty for being chiefly moral force; and adorned by a spirit of holiness and tender sympathy, which is most abundant in those who have striven most to follow Christ's example. Courage and strength are as truly courage and strength when they are exercised without deeds of violence. Thus when Bishop Patteson landed unarmed on the shores of Pacific Islands, crowded with ferocious savages, and, by the mere dignity of his presence and fearless bearing, won their submission to his will, and persuaded them to entrust to his care the children of their chiefs to be educated, he was gaining a victory as real, and far more noble, than if he had defeated them in battle. And thus we can trace in the life of our Lord and Saviour Jesus Christ the essential qualities which made Samson memorable, purged of the stains which marred Samson's character. Our Lord's ministry on earth was the exercise of a spiritual power by which He subdued to Himself the forces of nature, and the stubborn will of man. The stormy sea, the tempest, the manifold diseases of mind and body, death itself, all yielded to His word. Only on His own behalf He wrought no miracle. His wonder-working power was administered as a trust on behalf of mankind. No more emphatic contrast can be imagined than that between the blind vindictive champion of Israel, putting forth his last effort of strength to crush his enemies, and the Saviour of the world, the true light of Israel, with arms outstretched on the Cross, praying "Father, forgive them, for they know not what they do." We are often tempted to despond at the slow progress of Christ's kingdom in the hearts of men. If we look back to the life of Samson, we may find some encouragement, viewing it as a landmark which we have left behind. Some progress, at all events, the Church of Christ has made, by God's grace, since a character like Samson's was regarded as a standard for imitation; and if any now take such a standard for themselves, they are not among the true followers of Christ. His Gospel has raised a standard of holiness and charity, compared with which the fine gold of the world is dross.

For our part, brethren, let us endeavour to use our gifts of whatever kind, whether great or small, whether private or national, according to the spirit of Christ: that is, not for vain glory or selfish ends, but for the service of God and man. Value moral courage, patience, and self-control, above physical courage; holiness more than strength, forgiveness more than vengeance. Look away from the heroes who have been as destroying angels, to Him who died to save the world. It is a great work to pull down the Temple of Dagon single-handed. It is a greater to help even as a labourer, in building the Church of the living God.

XIII. BOAZ.

"Boaz came from Bethlehem and said unto the reapers, The Lord be with you. And they answered him, The Lord bless thee."—*Ruth* ii. 4.

(𝕳𝖆𝖗𝖛𝖊𝖘𝖙 𝕿𝖍𝖆𝖓𝖐𝖘𝖌𝖎𝖛𝖎𝖓𝖌.)

OUR faith directs us to Holy Scripture for lessons of godliness under every kind of circumstances. The common incidents of private life, birth, marriage, sickness, death: the public events of war, treaties of peace, the accession of sovereigns: the secret experiences which each soul keeps to itself, all find alike a feeling record in the Bible. We look there for sympathy on the most various occasions, and never in vain. Whatever concerns us is touched in some portion of God's word, and touched with a penetrating wisdom which moves our inmost hearts.

The book of Ruth, short as it is, is rich in examples of the beauty of holiness in domestic life. It is a picture or idyll, representing the manners of the children of Israel in the days which followed their possession of the promised land.

The incidents turn on the harvest of the fertile cornfields of Bethlehem, the "House of Bread," for such is the interpretation of the name. We are thus led to contemplate a scene which though ancient is ever fresh, the gathering in of the fruits of the earth by which our life is sustained.

Elsewhere we read much of wars and deeds of violence at this period. From the books of Joshua, Judges, and Samuel, we might suppose that human life in the days of Ruth and Boaz was a state of continual bloodshed, destroying and being destroyed, oppression and rapine. We are told how the Midianites carried away the crops for plunder, how Samson burned those of the Philistines, how the Israelites were compelled to go down to the Philistine cities to find a smith to sharpen their ploughshares. We turn a brighter page of history in the book of Ruth. For there we read of seasons of peace and plenty in Israel. Notwithstanding the disorder of the times, there were men who lived to row old in prosperous agriculture, and in habits of piety and righteousness. Such a one was Boaz, the ancestor of David, and of our Saviour Jesus Christ.

The simple words of the text relate that his custom during harvest was to go down and visit his reapers, greeting them at their work. He would say, "The Lord be with you," and they would answer, "The Lord bless thee." Characteristic sayings, which would not have been recorded if they had not been descriptive of the mutual relation of the master and his servants. This brief interchange of blessings is a sign of faith in the living God, and of kindly fellowship. We infer that Boaz and his reapers lived in the fear of the Lord, confessing His name with honest frankness, and invoking His blessing on each other with mutual good-will. Men spoke as they felt in that primitive age. Words had not yet become unmeaning by conventional use, like coin defaced by wear, but came fresh from the heart. The master desired God's blessing on his servants, the servants on their master. We cannot imagine a happier state than such concord hallowed by worship. Would that we all might enter more fully into the spirit of this interchange of blessings, when we re-echo them in our Church Services, when the minister says "The Lord be with you," and the people reply, "And with thy spirit."

The worth of this example endures for all time. Now, as of old, it is right for labour and capital to join together in holy fellowship. The master should desire that God's blessing may be on the men whose toil is contributing to his prosperity, and they in their turn should wish for God's blessing on their employer. The spirit of intercession on either side is the very salt of life. If there be any who hold that the changes of modern society have made antiquated the example of Boaz, they have not well considered the eternal laws of God. Shallow observation may lead us to think of the fellowship of master and men as a bygone virtue. But we can see by deeper reflection that the bond which connects them is permanent and everlasting. Masters and men are members of one social body. If the whole body prospers, it must be through the prosperity of the members, all together. It may be that in some particulars the interest of one conflicts with that of another: but the interests which all have in common are greater than the separate interests of any. Thus a labourer will sometimes think that his wages are less than his due, and demand more; while the master on the other hand thinks the claim excessive and unfair. Hence arises disputing, discontent, perhaps a strike, with much loss and suffering on both sides, which would be spared if, in considering their private interest, they took a larger view. That which causes bitterness in questions of capital and labour is the want of consideration for the body as a whole. It is the want of a spirit such as we see in Boaz and his harvestmen, each wishing well to the other. In old times, as now, there were selfish men and selfish masters. Isaiah speaks of elders and princes who grind the faces of the poor. We read of rich men who oppress the poor in his wages, and we read also of lawless men who rise in revolt against their masters. The story of Nabal is an instance of both. All history, and particularly Jewish history, is a record of such conflicts. The oppression of Israel in Egypt, and the revolt of the northern tribes under Jeroboam, are the chief examples among many. Thus it is no new phenomenon, peculiar to our day, if we hear of disputes between class and class, between employer and employed. The hard necessities of life have always given occasion to such disputes; and the temper in which they are adjusted must depend on the godly or ungodly spirit of the opposing parties. Prudence will do much, but not everything. Above prudence is the spiritual motive of faith in God. He calls us to live, not for ourselves, but for Him, not by a narrow rule of private interest or class-interest, but by self-devotion to the welfare of the whole body to which we belong, because "we being many, are one body in Christ, and every one members one of another."

There have been large employers of labour in our own day, such as the late Mr. Brassey, who have reconciled the patriarchal spirit of Boaz with the conditions of modern trade.

Doubtless it may be said, that when masters and men are familiarly acquainted with each other, living in the same parish, and worshipping in the same Church, there is more to keep alive a sense of fellowship, than in huge towns where fellow-workers lose sight of each other in a multitude. It may also be said with truth, that the relations of master and man are less cordial on either side, when it is felt that they have not to deal personally with one another, but are more or less pledged to an organized association of their own class. These are real and grave hindrances to the fulfilment of such an ideal of social brotherhood as the text sets before us. But let us not lose faith in the natural bonds of neighbourly kindness, still less in the grace of the Holy Spirit. If we have greater difficulties than Boaz, we have also greater means of grace.

The Spirit of Christ is essentially a Spirit of fellowship, without limit of class, or locality, or nation. Under His influence the employer will at all events wish well for his workmen, and they for him. So the prayers, "The Lord be with you," "the Lord bless thee," will rise mutually, even among the sharpest contentions, and surely where this spirit is, disputes will lose much of their asperity.

Wherever the Spirit of Christ is, His presence must needs be felt in some measure as a living active power, striving against the impulses of selfishness and passion. I am far from saying that a man is no Christian, because he is not always obedient to the Holy Spirit. All I would say is that, if we are Christians more than in name only, we shall bear some fruit unto God. Some movement of spiritual grace in our souls there will be, to make us more just, more patient, more charitable, than we should be if we had never heard of Christ.

There are a few, a very few, of whom it can be said, as it was said of St. Stephen, that they are "full of the Holy Ghost," their whole character animated with spiritual life. Of a larger number we may say that, although they are subject to human frailty, they do in some measure give evidence in their lives that they have not received the grace of God in vain. Under His blessed influence they bear the fruits of the Spirit, not indeed ripely, nor in perfection, yet so as to make it manifest that they are sealed as the servants of the Lord Jesus.

The text and subject which I have brought before you has a special appropriateness to the season of harvest. It was at harvest-time that Boaz went down to his fields, to overlook the reapers. It is at harvest-time that in all agricultural districts the goodwill of masters and men is drawn forth most abundantly. And there is a true connexion between a spirit of thankfulness to God for His bounty to us, and a spirit of fellowship towards neighbours who are beholden to Him, as we are.

Solemn thanksgiving for harvest formed a part of the religious services of the Old Covenant. In Deuteronomy, xvi. 15, it is written, "Because the Lord thy God shall bless thee in all thine increase, and in all the works of thine hands, therefore thou shalt surely rejoice."

The great feast of Pentecost was originally a harvest festival. Its period was reckoned by numbering seven weeks from the time when the sickle was put to the corn. New associations, more sacred than the first, hallowed the day of Pentecost in connexion with the giving of the Law. Yet the festival was always distinguished by the offering of two wheaten loaves. And this original significance of Pentecost as a Harvest Feast was fulfilled in a spiritual sense by the descent of the Holy Ghost at Whitsuntide, when a harvest of human souls, the first fruits of the Christian Church, was gathered in by the power of the Spirit through the ministry of the Apostles, preaching salvation through Christ.

Genuine thanksgiving for God's gifts involves the observance of two great and sacred laws: the law of temperance, and the law of charity. We must use the gifts of God with temperance, in order that we may offer to Him sincere and acceptable thanks for them. When we look upon the face of the land enriched by God's bounteous favour, when we see the cornfields spread out like a golden sea before our eyes, we thank God without reserve for His gift of daily bread, as a means of life, and health, and happiness. But it is with mingled feelings that we must look upon the vineyards terraced along the sunny hill-sides, or upon the luxuriant growth of the hop-gardens. These also are

God's gifts, and we can thank Him for them if we use them well. But how shall we presume to offer thanks to the Almighty for gifts abused? The thankfulness which turns to intemperance and excess, is indeed a mockery of God. Better far that the choicest fruits of the earth should be renounced, as if they were hemlock and nightshade, than that they should be used to debase and brutalize the image of God in man.

A second law, which is dictated by genuine thanksgiving, is charity: that we should for gratitude to God endeavour to please Him by such acts of loving service to our brethren as He delights in. There are many channels in which our charity can flow. It has always appeared to me that the fittest object of Harvest Thank-offerings, is the ministry of the Bread of Life, in one or other of its various forms. Our Lord Jesus Christ, as He looked on the cornfields, thought of the perishing souls of men, and said, "The harvest truly is great, but the labourers are few: pray ye therefore the Lord of the harvest, that He will send forth labourers into His harvest."

Boaz, taking pity on the Gentile Ruth, is a type of Christ showing compassion on the heathen of all the earth, giving them first the gleanings of His field, and afterwards admitting them to the fullness of adoption, as joint members of the Church, which is His Body.

As we ponder on the thoughts of harvest, they supply deeper and wider subjects of meditation. We begin by considering simply the gift of daily bread, and other benefits of the same kind, by which our natural life is sustained and cheered. Then, as we reflect more deeply, we call to mind that man doth not live by bread alone. We learn to acknowledge the spiritual food by which our souls are nourished, the word of God, and the Sacrament of Christ's Body and Blood. Further, we are led on by God's Spirit to survey that great harvest unreaped as yet, the field of Christ's Missions at home and abroad. Finally we look forward to that greater harvest which shall be the consummation of all things, when angels will be the reapers. May we, brethren, so use the bounties of God in our present life, that we may be found ripe for that great day. May the gifts which he has conferred upon us, and which we too often forget, our meat and drink, our health, our education, our talents, our opportunities, all combine to make us fruitful in every good word and work, to the praise of His holy name.

XIV. SAUL.

"Thy kingdom shall not continue."
1 *Samuel* xiii. 14.

(**Fourth Sunday after Trinity,** P.M.)

AMONG the "hard sentences of old," which exercise our minds and hearts in the study of Holy Scripture, is the condemnation pronounced by Samuel, in God's name, upon the first king of Israel. The rejection of Saul appears at first sight a punishment out of due proportion to his fault; and it is only by examination of the whole story in a reverent spirit that we can reconcile to our conscience, for our own practical instruction, the lesson which is taught us here.

Saul's first error was that he took upon himself the priest's office, after waiting in vain for Samuel. The case appeared to him one of necessity. Precious time was passing, his army was deserting, and the Philistines were near. These excuses were urged by Saul, with no want of respect, when Samuel arrived immediately after the sacrifice was offered. But the prophet gave a stern answer, "Thou hast done foolishly." "Thou hast not kept the commandment of the Lord thy God." "Thy kingdom shall not continue."

Severe as this warning was, it does not seem to have been more than a warning. If Saul had taken to heart the words of Samuel, and considered the strict obedience which God required of him, the door of forgiveness was not yet closed. We read in Ezekiel xxxiii. "When I say unto the wicked, thou shalt surely die, if he turn from his sin, and do that which is lawful and right, he shall surely live." Room for repentance was left to Saul, until a second and more wilful act of disobedience brought upon him the final sentence of rejection. Samuel charged him, in God's name, to make war upon Amalek, and utterly destroy the nation. According to the law of the Old Covenant, he was to spare neither man, woman, nor child, nor the flocks and herds of the Amalekites. This command Saul executed for the most part; but with two notable exceptions. He spared the King of Amalek, and the best of the sheep and oxen. In considering this history, we must keep in view the law of exclusiveness under which the Jewish nation had been formed, and we must not apply the rules of mercy, which a larger humanity teaches us under the New Covenant. God educates nations, like children, by gradual steps; and He willed in His wisdom to separate Israel from the heathen for their own spiritual training, and also to be executioners of His judgment.

We have to regard Saul's conduct simply in the light of a transgression against God's command. He disobeyed the word of God's inspired prophet; and the lesson of the history is summed up in the rebuke of Samuel:

"Hath the Lord as great delight in burnt
    offerings and sacrifices,
as in obeying the voice of the Lord?
Behold, to obey is better than sacrifice,
and to hearken than the fat of rams.
For rebellion is as the sin of witchcraft,
and stubbornness is as iniquity and idolatry.
Because thou hast rejected the word of the Lord,
He hath also rejected thee from being king."

From that time forward a gloom overspread the reign of Saul, and his own soul; the presence of Samuel was withdrawn from him, and with him he felt that God's favour was withdrawn. Soon the Philistines threatened his kingdom. They were defeated; but the glory of the victory was won by the young champion David; and when Saul heard the Jewish maidens extolling David above himself, he felt that he was losing the popularity for which he had been willing to disobey God's command. Then he fell into a dark and dangerous melancholy. "The Spirit of the Lord departed from him, and an evil spirit from the Lord troubled him." He attempted David's life. He stained his own good fame, and broke the plighted faith of the nation, by a massacre of the Gibeonites. He became suspicious of the loyalty of the priests, and massacred them also. At last, forsaking utterly his better courses, he resorted to magic, and strove in despair to hold converse with the ghost of Samuel. His end was the end of the desperate, namely suicide.

Many lessons are suggested by Saul's career, and we must be careful to interpret faithfully what is set down in the Bible. If we use the Scriptures like an instrument of music, opening them here, and closing them there, that they may sound what note we please, we shall fail to hear in them the genuine voice by which God speaks to us.

That Saul was rejected for disobedience is the obvious lesson of his history; and this lesson comes home to us with more emphatic force when we observe that his disobedience was in every case veiled by some fair pretext. He was not a defiant transgressor of God's law, like Ahab. On the contrary, he professed absolute obedience to God, and respect for Samuel as God's minister. His behaviour towards Samuel is as deferential as that of kings of the Middle Ages towards the Popes, when they went at the Papal summons to a Crusade. If Saul presumed so far as to offer sacrifice, he could plead that it was not of his own will, but under force of circumstances. If he left the destruction of Amalek incomplete, he could plead that such was the wish of the people. Plausible excuses, through which the prophet saw the undisciplined, rebellious spirit of the man, which was afterwards to be manifested more openly. His acts, judged according to the superficial view of human judgment, were easily to be pardoned, if not altogether to be defended: but the penetrating eye of Samuel read in his heart more than the actions immediately disclosed. We have, therefore, an illustration in Saul not only of God's judgment on disobedience, but of the searching severity of that judgment, piercing through the armour of excuses and subterfuges to the very heart. And this is one of the most valuable lessons to be drawn for our own conduct, from Saul's downfall. Let us keep in mind that God reads our hearts and lays bare the secret thoughts of which we are scarcely conscious. Beware of the perilous facility of making excuses for not doing what God bids; lest, instead of concealing your fault, you only blind your own eyes to the knowledge of yourself.

Observe also in Saul another quality so plausible that it looks like a virtue, and did in fact deceive himself. He was forward, and even eager, in the voluntary service of God. Twice he incurred blame by his zealous desire to offer sacrifice; first, when he took Samuel's place, and afterwards, when he let the people reserve the best of the sheep and oxen. So he drew upon himself that admonition, which is for all men, and for all time, that "to obey is better than sacrifice." How many are ready to offer to God anything they have, rather than simple obedience! We like to do service to God in a form which does not fetter our liberty; to exercise a free will in our worship. So, in the present day, devout men and women are often impatient of the duties which God's voice dictates to them, and would fain take their own way of honouring Him. Zealous, yet self-willed in their zeal, they wish to please Him by some spontaneous sacrifice after their own fashion; not considering what He desires, but only what they wish to offer. Brethren, if you wish indeed to please God, it must be by doing His will, as He has revealed it. No liberality to the poor, however profuse, no gifts to the Church, or voluntary actions of religion, can condone the breach of God's plain laws of justice, mercy, and truth.

What we read concerning Saul is the more significant, when we consider that he was the first who held the office of King in Israel. He was the first of God's chosen people to stand

> "In that fierce light which beats upon a throne
> And blackens every blot."

The example of his conduct was of enormous influence to his people. As yet, no custom or traditional precedent had fixed the limits of the royal power, and the relation of the king to the Divine law and the priesthood. Saul's transgressions were therefore not simple isolated faults, but examples for generations to come, authoritative precedents of disobedience, if they had passed unrebuked.

It was the will of the people to have a king. Samuel foresaw the dangers which accompanied such a wish, the inherent dangers of royalty; that a man, exalted far above his fellows, would forget his allegiance to God, and would take an arbitrary course without regard to the law and constitution of the kingdom; that the people also would lose the consciousness of having God for their king, and raise their thoughts no higher than His human deputy. All this was before the mind of Samuel, and he appealed to God in prayer before he consented to the people's desire. Having complied with their wish, he strove to guard against the perils which he foresaw. With a holy jealousy he asserted the majesty of God against the majesty of man, and denounced fearlessly the king's infraction of God's command.

In the history of Saul his faults are brought so prominently before us, that we are apt to think too little of those other features of his character which make his example the more instructive by drawing our human sympathy towards him. If, however, we look back to his early days, and survey his life as a whole, from its hopeful dawn to its stormy sunset, we shall find few lives more deeply interesting. There is in him that mixture of good and bad, of noble impulso and calamitous error, which forms the tragedy of life, making us admire and pity while we blame. Saul was indeed no mean, no ordinary prince. When he first stood before Samuel there lay hid behind his reserved manner the fire of a character which his nearest kinsmen suspected not; and the spirit within him, stirred to its depths by the calling and anointing which he received, was displayed by an enthusiasm which amazed them. "Is Saul among the prophets?" was an exclamation of wonder which became a proverb; so great was the change in him, when he met the prophets at Gibeah, and was inspired with a gift of utterance like theirs. Again his natural bashfulness returned, when he was elected king, and he was found hidden among the baggage of the camp. But his election was immediately justified by the aptitude which he showed for war and government. His gigantic figure was not more distinguished above common men, than the energy of his mind. His valour, tried at once by the invasion of the Ammonites, was so prompt and decisive, that before mid-day there were not two of the enemy left together. He proceeded to adorn his victory by an act of royal clemency towards those who had thought him unworthy of the kingdom. The people would have had them slain, but he said, "There shall not a man be put to death this day, for to-day the Lord hath wrought salvation in Israel." On every side he fought victoriously, and the surrounding nations found him an adversary more formidable than they had known since the days of Joshua.

In the midst of this career of success the weakness of his character begins to show itself. His hasty words and actions, his rashness in making a vow which nearly cost the life of Jonathan, his impatience of Samuel's delay, all show a mind which is governed by impulse, not by principle. For want of fixed and steadfast principle his conduct is inconsistent, at one time indulgent, at another cruelly severe. Thus, while sparing Agag, he slew the Gibeonites. While seeking to take the life of David, he was moved on a sudden by David's generosity, to ask his pardon. After trying to destroy all the dealers in magic, he goes himself to consult a witch. Human nature has few spectacles more affecting than the wreck of a noble character through instability of purpose. To see a man whose impulses have been once high and generous, labouring in vain, like a good ship without a rudder aimlessly drifting to and fro, is a sight to bring tears even to manly eyes. But never is the spectacle so full of pity as when the mind, unstayed by the Spirit of God, falls a prey to the evil spirits of jealousy and melancholy. As we follow the life of Saul through his long and miserable reign, to the closing scene on the hill of Gilboa, we read a tragedy, the natural pathos of which has been illustrated by the genius of Alfieri in verse, and of Handel in music, but which no art can make more touching than it is in fact. If you have known anyone whose rashness and impulsiveness have set God's law at nought, and brought down the hopes of a generous youth to the despair of a dishonoured old age, you will sympathize in that pathetic elegy, in which David bewails the death of the once mighty king who formerly had loved him well.

One point is to be noted in conclusion. The obedience which God requires is not a punctilious adherence to formal rules, but a loyal submission of will. Where the soul is loyal to God, all commands and ordinances are merged in one commandment of love. We have, even in the Old Testament and in the days of Saul, an instructive example of the breadth of God's commandment, in the case of David eating the shew-bread. Our Lord Jesus Christ refers to this in illustration of the freedom of the Sabbath for uses of charity, and lays down the rule that "the Sabbath was made for man, and not man for the Sabbath." But we need a clear conscience and a single eye to God's glory, to be fair judges of a case of necessity. In nothing are we more apt to be led astray by the impulses of nature, it may be kindly and even religious impulses, but to be resisted so far as they shake the first principles of loyalty to God. What we admire in the young as elements of a heroic character, bold, quick, and generous impulses, need to be controlled and governed by an inflexible law of duty. Failing this, the early promise of childhood bears no fruit, and withers unprofitably away. The Spirit of Christ, which is the spirit of love to God, is not under the law; but it is by obedience to God's law that we learn to love Him. "I will walk at liberty: for I seek Thy commandments." Through practice of well-doing comes that love of well-doing which is perfect spiritual freedom.

XV. DAVID.

"The Lord seeth not as man seeth: for man looketh on the outward appearance, but the Lord looketh on the heart."—1 *Samuel* xvi. 7.

(*Fifth Sunday after Trinity*, P.M.)

TO see through outward appearances to the heart, to penetrate beyond illusion to truth, is a Divine gift of inestimable value. According to Oriental philosophy, this stands as the definition of the end and aim of human life. If we can by any means attain to it, the pains we take will be well repaid; but in every case the discovery of that which is, of hidden truth, is to some extent a revelation, a lifting of the veil which intervenes between man and God.

Samuel was thus guided to the choice of David for King of Israel. Sent with a secret commission to anoint one of the sons of Jesse of Bethlehem, he caused the young men to pass in order before him. As he saw the first, Eliab, a tall and handsome soldier, he said within himself, "Surely the Lord's anointed is here." Doubtless he remembered the day when God had directed him to anoint Saul. Now, after the lapse of thirty years, he saw such another prince of nature's royalty. But the Lord warned the aged prophet, by that voice which he had learned from childhood to recognize and obey, that this was not the man whom He had chosen. So Eliab passed by, and Abinadab, and Shammah, and four more brothers, and at length Samuel asked of Jesse, "Are here all thy children?" One was still absent, the youngest, who kept the sheep. Jesse sent for him, and as he approached, the Lord said, "Arise, anoint him, for this is he."

The youth on whom God's choice fell was known in his family by the name of David, or darling. His early promise and the favour of his parents drew upon him the envy of his brothers, who took pleasure in slighting him, and treating him as a boy. To outward appearance he was little more. Strange it is, indeed, to place ourselves in fancy among Jesse's household, and to look as with Samuel's eyes upon the scene; to behold the young shepherd entering hastily from the field at the prophet's awful summons, with glowing cheek and flashing eye; to reflect on the heroic valour, the poetical genius, the royal majesty, which were to be manifested afterwards in him; and to know further, as we know, that the heart which beat in his youthful breast was not only large enough to embrace the cares of the kingdom of Israel, but deep enough to supply language of praise and prayer for ages to come. David's Psalms were to be the fittest utterance of all religious emotion, from the daily hymns of little children, to the agony of the Redeemer on the Cross. Souls more stainless have been inspired by the Holy Ghost, but none more susceptible of the grace of life, more rich in spiritual vitality. The heart of David, which God saw, when Samuel saw only his countenance, was afterwards to undergo trials of prosperity and adversity almost unparalleled, and to issue from this ordeal a potent factor in the history of mankind. His life fills a large space in the Old Testament, and the impress of his character can be traced, not only on the Jewish nation, but on all Christendom. To mention only one instance: his generous respect for Saul, as "the Lord's anointed," is an example of loyalty, which was constantly before the minds of the adherents of the kings of the house of Stuart during the troubles of the Civil War and afterwards. They learned from David to hold sacred the person of their sovereign.

Fully as the acts of David are recorded, we have some difficulty in forming a just idea of his varied character. Even now, as at first when Samuel saw him, there are outward appearances to be put aside, in order to see the man as he really was. We have to guard on the one hand against the fascination of his valour, which the maidens of Israel felt when they sang his praises, and the charm of his minstrelsy, which touched the heart of Saul. On the other hand, we have to guard against the bias which affects us, in regarding him from the point of view of modern Christian civilization, and makes us amazed at the bloodshed and the treachery by which his life is conspicuously marked.

The first step to a right understanding of David's character is to conceive distinctly the state of society in which he grew up. We must look to the outlawed Macgregors of Rob Roy's day for a parallel to the ferocious manners of the children of Israel in his youth. Nor does this comparison adequately represent to us all the circumstances: a mountain region infested by wild beasts, where the shepherd had to defend his flock from lions and bears, a land where life and property were exposed alternately to foreign invasion, and to the attacks of such marauding parties as we read of in the stories of Micah and the Benjamites, in the book of Judges. It was the work of David's reign to establish some good order in this wild state, to obtain some reverence for God's laws of justice and mercy, and for solemn religious worship : to make the royal power a terror to evil-doers, and an encouragement to those who did well. That in these circumstances he sometimes transgressed the laws which he strove to enforce is not wonderful. We shall rather wonder that he was in the main so true to his ideal of the office of a king.

Several of the Psalms were written at a time when he was a captain of outlaws, when his life was in danger alike from Saul and the Philistines, and his fame as a warrior had drawn to him " every one that was in distress, and every one that was in debt, and every one that was discontented." To these banditti he teaches lessons of piety and chivalry to which they were little accustomed. He bids them refrain their tongues from evil, and their lips that they speak no guile. The gentleness of his followers wins praise from the servants of the churlish Nabal. Twice he foregoes his own advantage, and lets Saul escape him. Another touching sign of his greatness of heart is the incident at Bethlehem, when he refused to drink the water which had been brought to him by three of his companions by a desperate act of valour. He poured it out solemnly as a sacrifice, and said, "Be it far from me, O Lord: is not this the blood of the men that went in jeopardy of their lives?" Such chivalrous touches of character explain the power by which he won the hearts of all men. They would be beautiful in a Christian soldier of our own time; but they stand out with singular brightness from the dark background of a life like David's. Towards the Philistines he acted with a deceit and fierceness which we can hardly excuse, consistent as it was with the stern exclusiveness of the Old Covenant. But we see David again at his best in his unswerving fidelity to Saul and Jonathan. Selfishness and worldly ambition would have suggested that he should turn against the king who had been a bitter enemy to him. Nevertheless, under all perils and temptations, he cherished the sacred duty of faithfulness to God, to his king and his country. And when Saul and Jonathan fell together on Mount Gilboa, David lamented them with a generous sorrow, which recalled only the lovely and pleasant aspects of their memory.

New fields of enterprise opened to David on his accession to the throne of Israel. He took the mountain fortress of Jerusalem, hitherto impregnable, but henceforward the centre of Jewish national life, and for all time to come the symbol of social order, based on the worship of the one true God. The Ark was brought to Mount Zion, with enthusiasm of joy at the completion of the conquest of the promised land; and preparations were made for the building of the Temple, for a permanent sanctuary of the Lord God Almighty, "exceeding magnifical."

David's organizing power raised Israel speedily to a mighty kingdom, stretching out its dominion, like the cords of a tent, into adjacent lands. While his victories struck terror into the nations on every side, he busied himself with the establishment of orderly government, appointing officers of justice, collectors of the revenue, and so forth. In the later years of his reign he assumed something of the state of an Eastern Sultan, with evil consequences to himself and to his house.

One great crime, committed in the licence of despotic power, is memorable even more for his repentance than for his guilt. Absolute monarchs, in ancient and modern times, have so often set themselves above all law, that we cannot but admire the king who bowed himself meekly under the prophet's rebuke, acknowledging that he had sinned in taking Uriah's wife, and causing him to be slain by the children of Ammon. David was surrounded by a bodyguard of soldiers who were ready, at a sign from him, to despatch anyone who offended him. But Nathan's parable brought him to his better self, and he confessed his sin in words which have served as a model of penitent prayer, the words of the 51st Psalm. His prayer was granted. God did not cast him out from His presence, nor take His Holy Spirit from him.

Reviewing as a whole the course of David's life, as it is recorded in the books of Samuel and Chronicles, there is one feature of character which strikes us even more than the splendour of his varied gifts. It is not the greatness or the goodness of the man which strikes us most, for history relates the acts of founders of empires on a larger scale, and men in all stations have more nearly fulfilled his own description of the righteous, "He that hath clean hands, and a pure heart." What is specially characteristic of David is the warmth of his affection towards God and man, so that we might apply to him the words, "His sins, which were many, are forgiven, for he loved much." God was to him a "shepherd," his "hope and strength," his "buckler," the "horn of his salvation," and his "refuge." No man, perhaps, has ever lived in whom the consciousness of God's presence was more vivid, or the hunger and thirst for righteousness more intense. With this personal affection for God was combined a remarkable warmth of heart, in every social relation. While the love of David for Jonathan is a pattern of friendship, his love for Absalom has a pathetic tenderness which moves us, in spite of its excess, as an example of fatherly affection. His nature was one which overflowed in love, and inspired a similar love in the hearts of others.

The practical lesson of David's life may be gathered up in one sentence, which is full of encouragement to those who need encouragement most. It is, that God can be served in every condition of life, however unfavourable to godliness. David's experience comprises the trials of extreme hardship and the more insidious temptations of prosperity. Called from the sheepfold to the camp and court, then an outlaw and a companion of outlaws, associated with men of ruined fame and fortune, an exile among the Philistines, then raised to the giddy height of royal power, he found means throughout to keep his ears open to that heavenly music in which God speaks to those who are willing to hear. Therefore any man may be sure that his hindrances, whatever they may be, are not such as to exclude him from the highest privileges of the kingdom of heaven. Do not say that your business, or your family cares, or your social surroundings, make holiness impossible to you. David's acceptance with God is a pledge of His merciful allowance for the circumstances in which you are placed. God will judge each one of us, not according to the superficial standards of human judgment, but looking to the heart, with perfect understanding of our trials, our opportunities, and our efforts. In the last great day, in which all nations shall be gathered before the throne of Christ, many that are first shall be last, and many that are last shall be first. The miserable inequalities of the present life will be adjusted. Those who seemed here to have no chance of turning to good, brought up in the company of profane and vicious comrades, will not be of necessity classed with them; for the all-seeing eye of the Judge will discern in them any striving towards a purer life. Those whom we are apt to censure freely, at the highest and lowest extremities of society—the rich, tempted to sin through self-indulgence, the poor, tempted to crime by wretchedness—are both alike sure of an equitable sentence, according to a more righteous award than we can make. If God has hedged us round by His providence, and sustained us by His grace, so that our temptations are less, and our conduct more irreproachable, than those of the mighty men of old, let us not suppose that we are better than they or their living counterparts. Passionless perfection is not so much after God's own heart, as a heart like that of David, or that of St. Peter, which can appeal to the Searcher of hearts and say, "Lord, thou knowest all things, thou knowest that I love thee."

The scene of Samuel anointing David has a suggestive counterpart in the New Testament. When the infant Saviour was brought into the presence of an inspired prophet, the aged Simeon, and received his blessing, the world knew Him not. Pharisees were parading their spurious virtues and debating petty subtleties of law, princes of the house of Herod were astonishing the citizens of Jerusalem by aping the imperial pomp of Rome, when a poor woman entered the Temple gates to return thanks for the birth of her first-born son. Little did the visitors to the Temple suspect who it was that was borne through the crowd. But the Spirit of God whispered to Simeon, who had been waiting prayerfully for the Messiah, the Lord's Anointed, "Arise, for this is He." So the old man rose, trembling with awe but not with doubt, and received into his arms the sacred burden of the King of kings and Lord of lords.

For us the mystery of the Incarnation is virtually renewed, whenever our duty to Christ presents itself in a lowly, insignificant form. We have before our eyes some task of no outward show of importance, but commended to us by the voice of God within our conscience; it may be the care of a child, or the nursing of a sick person, or the daily labour of the hands: and herein we have Christ present with us, to try the sincerity of our devotion. He says, "Inasmuch as ye did it to one of the least of these, ye did it unto Me." Whether the sphere of our duty be large or small is of little consequence in God's sight. Few men in a generation can fill such a space as to achieve what the world calls greatness. A career like David's must of necessity be rare. Indeed, in some important respects he stands alone in history. But the weakest and least among the true servants of Christ can win the blessing, "Thou hast been faithful in a few things, I will make thee ruler over many things."

XVI. RIZPAH.

" There was a famine in the days of David three years, year after year; and David enquired of the Lord. And the Lord answered, It is for Saul, and for his bloody house, because he slew the Gibeonites."—2 *Samuel* xxi. 1.

TWO severe calamities, beside the revolt of Absalom, troubled the later years of David's reign. A famine of three years, and a pestilence of three days, were sent by God for punishment of certain public transgressions. In each case the sin was committed by one man, though it involved the whole nation. The famine was because of Saul, the pestilence was because of David. We are shown in both events the operation of that Divine law, which binds together for good or evil the several members of society, the parents and their children, the people and their king.

The history of the famine is one of the most remarkable instances in Holy Scripture of this mysterious law. It is, besides, a story full of interest and sadness. During Saul's reign there lived among the children of Israel, in a servile condition, a race belonging to the old stock of the nations of Canaan, whom God commanded His people to root out. This race of people, the Gibeonites, would have been extirpated by Joshua, had he not solemnly sworn that their lives should be spared. For they came to him after the fall of Jericho and Ai, with old garments, worn out shoes, and mouldy bread, pretending to have made a long journey to seek his alliance. The princes of the congregation believed them, and rashly took an oath to let them live. Only two days after, the army of Joshua came to their city, in the very heart of the land of Canaan. But he respected the oath which had been taken. He let them live, though for punishment of their fraud he made them hewers of wood and drawers of water.

So they continued until the days of Saul; and Saul, as we read, "sought to slay them in his zeal to the children of Israel and Judah." We can recognize in this brief record of his crime the same character which appears throughout his life. The same impulsive disposition which led him to transgress the commands which God gave by Samuel, shows itself here in a breach of the solemn oath of the nation. The same desire for popularity which made him spare the choicer part of the spoil of the Amalekites, moved him here in the opposite direction to a deed of bloodshed. His motive was "zeal to the children of Israel and Judah." Neither the time nor the circumstances of the massacre are related; and the fact seems to have almost passed away from remembrance, until the famine came year after year, for three years. A new generation was occupied with new concerns, when Israel was reminded by a great affliction that a great wrong was crying for redress. When the harvest failed for the third time, leaving the people in such distress as we have heard of in our own day in the famines of India and China, such distress as is vividly described in the history of Elijah, and again in that of Elisha, then King David inquired of the Lord, probably through one of the prophets, and he was told, "It is for Saul and for his bloody house, because he slew the Gibeonites."

Let us try to represent to ourselves clearly the purport of this oracle, that we may better understand the law of judgment which it implies. In the last reign, so it was declared, the king had violated a sacred oath, and therefore the nation suffered. What makes this oracle of God the more surprising is, that the oath which had been broken was an oath plighted in ignorance four centuries ago, to a people who had been accursed by God, and had obtained the promise of life by deceit. Nevertheless, the lapse of time, and the deceit and demerit of the Gibeonites, were not to be pleaded in excuse for a breach of faith. Moreover, the sin was accounted a national sin. The nation by its representatives had taken the name of the Lord their God to witness, and the commandment stood fast for ever: "Thou shalt not take the name of the Lord thy God in vain." So when Saul as representative of the nation broke this promise, the transgression was national as the pledge had been. God "will not hold him guiltless that taketh his name in vain;" and the nation of Israel, which had overlooked, if not approved, the crime of the king, was brought to repentance by the visitation of hunger. He gave them "cleanness of teeth in all their cities, and want of bread in all their places."

The bond of social obligation which is shown here may appear strange to our notions. Yet it is in accordance with many plain facts of nature, and with the most ancient and universal ideas of mankind. If we compare two modern kingdoms, one prosperous, the other wretched, and inquire why the difference is, historians will point to events in the past, and say that the present generation have reaped what their forefathers have sown. Children inherit from their parents good and bad, blessings and curses.

The next part of the story of the Gibeonites puts this bond of kindred in the harshest and most repulsive form. David said to them, "What shall I do for you, and wherewith shall I make the atonement, that ye may bless the inheritance of the Lord?" The remnant of the Gibeonites, whose cries against the slayer of their brethren God had heard, were to choose their own atonement: and they would have no other compensation than the life of seven sons of Saul, the man who had "consumed" them. So vindictive a request might have been expected from heathen bondservants. What calls for serious reflection is, that the sacrifice of these innocent lives was granted by David, and apparently approved by God. "After that God was entreated for the land."

We have learned from the New Testament

a law of mercy, which bids us forgive, as we would be forgiven; which reprobates as horrible the thought of desiring the son's blood for the father's sin. We have also learned from the laws and customs of civilized lands a morality in some respects different from that of old time. One of the effects of civilization is to weaken family ties, and to separate each individual from his neighbours, making him answerable for his private acts alone. But this rule, good as it is for a principle of human law, relating to the affairs of man and man, takes only a partial view of the whole matter.

Jew and Gentile held in common certain maxims of natural right, which are illustrated in this history. To both the great maxim of criminal law is "Life for life." To both also the great maxim of civil law is, that man is a social being; that is to say, that each individual is a member of a family, or state, or society, with rights and obligations depending upon that social membership. Upon these two principles of natural justice the Gibeonites took their stand. Saul had shed their blood; therefore his blood was due for expiation. Saul's sons were his blood: therefore the sentence fell upon them. Such ideas of hereditary guilt are not peculiar to the Bible, or to the nations of which we read in the Bible. They may be illustrated from the early history of most races. For instance, in the great domestic war of the Greeks, the Peloponnesian war, the same principle was recognized in a notable manner. Each of the two contending parties accused the other of being polluted by guilt incurred in a former generation, which required expiation by the banishment of the descendants of the guilty.[1]

The humane legislation of Christian states forbears to exact full retributive justice, even upon the criminal himself. Much less do our laws involve children in the crime of their parents. And yet the children of the convicted felon suffer by the forfeiture of his goods. Nor is it possible by any means to prevent the inheritance of evil, which an infamous and vicious man leaves to his posterity. They draw from him a tainted name and tainted blood. David acted according to the primitive dictates of natural and revealed religion, when he delivered seven sons of Saul to the Gibeonites. They "hanged them in the hill before the Lord;" that is, as an expiatory sacrifice to God for

---

[1] Thucydides, B. P. i. 126.

their father's guilt. At this point of the narrative we are tempted to inquire, "Why has God made us to be answerable for the sins of others? Why are the oaths of our ancestors, and the misdeeds of our fathers, binding upon us without our own consent? What benefit is there in being bound by contract or by blood?" The Bible suggests an answer to such questions in the continuation of the same history.

Where we have so terrible an example of the penalties of family bonds, we have an example, most pathetic and beautiful, of the tender love by which the same family bonds are softened. We read how the mother of two of the men, Rizpah the daughter of Aiah, sat day and night on the rock watching the remains of her children, keeping from their corpses the foul birds of prey, and the beasts that came forth in the darkness. "She suffered neither the birds of the air to rest on them by day, nor the beasts of the field by night." Thus the bereaved woman kept her dreadful watch through the summer heat, until the rain came down, which showed that the sacrifice was accepted. Her patience and devotion, in fulfilling the last offices of a woman's love suggests a lifelong tale of motherly affection. She who was found so faithful to the ties of blood, under the unequal conditions of her lot, stands as an enduring proof of the blessedness of those ties. The example of love is an answer to anyone who murmurs against the law of social obligation, which makes one responsible for another's fault. The law, which visits the sin of the father on the children, has its compensation in the charities of domestic life, in the overflowing love, often disdained and unrequited, which guards our infancy, and alleviates the pains of sickness and the horrors of death. The privileges of sonship and the responsibilities of sonship go hand in hand, inseparable: and the Bible sets them here side by side, as if on purpose to show that the same Providence which visits the sins of the fathers upon the children, blesses the children abundantly through the parents' love.

David, hearing what Rizpah had done, was deeply moved. He went and took the bones of Saul and Jonathan from the city where they were preserved, and buried them with the bones of those that were hanged, in the sepulchre of Saul's family. He had done what retributive justice demanded, and his warm heart was never wanting in sympathy toward the house of his former king, and the bosom friend of his youth.

Considered as a whole, this history gives us, in a rude and primitive form, an outline of one great part of the plan by which God rules the world. The softer lights and shadows, by which Justice and Mercy are administered with discrimination to each individual soul, are wanting in this lurid picture. But it illustrates two great principles, which in their general application are true for all nations and all times. 1. That wrong requires atonement. 2. That families and nations are one body, knit together for benefit or for injury from generation to generation.

Many important conclusions follow from these principles, duly interpreted and applied to common life. But one is of supreme importance, being the foundation of all Christian faith and duty. Our spiritual condition by nature is a condition of hereditary guilt. As children of Adam we inherit our father's sin. The fault of the first parent became sin to the whole kind. All were conceived in sin, and by the law of inheritance shared Adam's curse, as they inherited also his image and his lordship over the creation. Though it was not possible for others to imitate Adam's fall from innocence, yet, being born sinful, the human race continued to sin, and required atonement both for their father's guilt and for their own. Yet on the other hand, the same law which was in Adam to condemnation, became in Christ a means of justification and of life eternal. Christ, being the Son of God and Son of Man, made on the Cross an atoning sacrifice for mankind; and He has further made us partakers of His salvation, by admitting us into the family of God. Thus a new bond of membership, with new privileges, is made to supersede the old. "As in Adam all die, even so in Christ shall all be made alive." Being born again of Water and of the Holy Ghost, we become members of Christ, coheirs with Him of His eternal glory. While our natural birth entails upon us the condition of our father Adam, our spiritual birth unites us in membership to Christ.

The same plan of vicarious atonement, in accordance with which the sons of Saul were hanged on the hill of Gibeah, was fulfilled by the sacrifice of Christ, lifted up on the Cross on the hill of Calvary. Concerning His death, the words of the former history may be repeated in a larger sense: "After that God was intreated for the land." The blood of the Lamb of God takes away the sin of the world.

It remains for us to hold fast the bond of

membership with Christ into which we are called. And while we imperil our own souls, if we forget God, there is to be borne in mind also the awful and mysterious danger we incur, that others whom we love may suffer through our fault. That chain of evil consequences which is vividly set before us in the career of the profligate, bringing misery and sickness upon children's children, runs on in many cases unperceived. As members of a family, and also as members of Christ's Church, the life that we lead is to a great extent shaped by that of others before us, and shapes to a great extent the lives of others after us. This reflection comes home with special force to those who are parents. God holds your children as hostages for your good behaviour. Their future welfare depends, not only on the education which you give them, but on the life which you personally lead. Thank God, while His judgment is measured, His mercy is unmeasured. He delights to show mercy unto thousands of them that love Him, and keep His commandments.

XVII. KING DAVID.

"Satan stood up against Israel, and provoked David to number Israel."—1 *Chronicles* xxi. 1.

(Seventh Sunday after Trinity, A.M.)

IN the corresponding passage of the book of Samuel we read, "The anger of the Lord was kindled against Israel, and he moved David against them to say, Go number Israel and Judah." By comparing together these two accounts we are led to infer that Satan, "the adversary," as his name signifies, was a minister of God for the chastisement of the nation of Israel and their king. Satan tempted David, and David was a rod in the hands of God to chastise Israel.

But why was it wrong to number the people? The answer to this question is not plain on the surface, and deserves the more careful consideration. No positive law was broken; on the contrary, the case was provided for in the law of Moses, and a poll-tax was to be levied, whenever the children of Israel were numbered. (Ex. xxx. 11, 12.) It was written, "They shall give every man a ransom for his soul unto the Lord, when thou numberest them; that there be no plague among them." Hence it has been supposed by some writers that the sin of David was a neglect to pay this tax. But we are not told so; and it is far better to interpret the lessons of Scripture, if possible, by what is recorded.

David himself was conscious that he had done wrong. His heart smote him, and he implored God for pardon. Perhaps there is nothing which so clearly proves the existence of a personal tempter, as the revulsion of feeling which follows, as soon as we have yielded to temptation. The spirit of evil hides from us the consequences of sin, till it is committed; then lifts the veil to mock us.

It is remarkable that Joab, the bold and treacherous captain of David's army, foreboded calamity from his master's command, and tried to dissuade him from his purpose. What moved his hard heart to such an apprehension we can only guess; it was probably the same natural sentiment, or we might almost call it instinct, which presages evil to come of boastfulness.

This fear is nearly allied to superstition, but it is not altogether superstitious. For it springs from the true principle that God judges the thoughts, and that pride is an offence against Him.

I think we must conclude that David's sin in numbering the people was that to which prosperous kings are most liable, the sin of pride. We may conceive his reflections to have been something like these:—

"Now I am King of Israel in peace, and all my enemies are subdued under me. I have triumphed over many rivals at home, and many foreign nations. Those whom I would I have destroyed, others I have made my servants, and put garrisons into their cities. Under me the children of Israel have entered into full possession of the promised land, flowing with milk and honey. My people have increased, like the stars of heaven, or the sands of the sea shore, according to God's promise to Abraham. Let me therefore count up the number of my people, and see how great a prince I am."

From a worldly point of view it may seem a venial fault to indulge in thoughts of this kind. For the world is apt to disregard sins against God, and reserve its blame for sins which concern our happiness in some immediate and practical consequence. A deed of aggression, committed under circumstances which make our lives insecure, is deemed a crime of the blackest character, whilst the sins of impiety and pride are almost unnoticed. Holy Scripture supplies a different measure of guilt. Moses lost his inheritance of the land of Canaan, by an angry blow upon the rock, and a few rash words which showed that he had forgotten his place as God's minister. In the New Testament, also, we read how Herod Agrippa was smitten with a strange and terrible death, because he accepted the flattery of the people, who praised his eloquence as the voice of a God.

These examples confirm the lesson of David's punishment for numbering the people, showing that our thoughts are under God's judgment. The most secret affections and desires which we entertain are subject to His eternal law ; and we mistake altogether the true proportions of good and bad conduct, if we take our measure from outward signs alone. If we drew no other lesson from this chapter of the history of Israel it would be well worthy of our thoughtful meditation, in order to fix in our minds that the inner life of our souls is under the searching eye of our Judge. The Lord Jesus Christ, Who sits in majesty at the Father's right hand, will judge our works, not only according to the appearance which they present to human eyes, but according to the thoughts and intents of our hearts. We know that His judgment will take merciful account of our frailty, and will not bear hardly upon us for involuntary thoughts of evil which Satan whispers in our ear. But for those deliberate thoughts which we adopt as our own with a consenting will, we must expect judgment, sooner or later. If you turn God's gifts to your own glory, saying, "This land, these houses, this money is mine," counting up your possessions and titles to honour, challenging comparisons with others less highly favoured, you will be sowing trouble to yourself in days to come. It is well for those who are led betimes to repentance through suffering, and are spared the curse of a hardened heart. Better the end of David than the end of Solomon.

There are, however, some special lessons which belong to the history of David's numbering the people, over and above the general law which it illustrates, of God's judgment of our thoughts. The scourge of the pestilence warns us against the fallacy of reckoning prosperity by mere numbers. Of what avail was it to David that he had fifteen hundred thousand men that drew sword, when the plague turned their strength into weakness? In the tainted air of the pestilence thousands and tens of thousands alike ceased to be of any account.

We are much exposed to this form of error. The gross measures of quantity are so much easier to ascertain than the quality of goodness or badness, that we are apt to be misled by them. In popular language a man is said to be "worth" so much, estimating his "worth" by the amount of his income. A nation's welfare is estimated by the population, the imports and exports, and other such things which can be computed in figures. Most of us hear with some pride the statistics which show the magnitude of the British Empire, how many hundred millions are subjects of our Queen, how far the population of London exceeds that of foreign cities. Let us not forget that there are surer standards of national prosperity than these, that the moral health of a city is more important than its numbers. If we consider how large a proportion of the inhabitants of London and other great cities are degraded by misery and vice, living in a state of heathenism the more gross for coming in contrast with Christian life in their neighbourhood, we must look upon the high figures of our census with anxiety rather than pride. We have cause to dread a pestilence, a moral pestilence of infidelity and sensuality, growing out of the very abundance of the numbers of our people, massed together without thought of God.

Neither by numbers nor by gold is the true wealth of nations to be measured. One thing is left untouched by all such statistics, the value of the souls of men; and this is by no means equal, though every soul is precious in God's sight. History, ancient and modern, abounds in examples which show that one man, or a few men, full of courage and faith, may be reckoned against thousands. From the Bible we may take such examples as Samson and Gideon. From Greek history we may take the Athenians who fought at Marathon, and the Spartans at Thermopylæ; from modern history, the Swiss mountaineers who overthrew the chivalry of Austria and Burgundy. These are instances in which moral character has been more than a match for numbers and riches combined in actual warfare. "The thicker the grass," said the fierce Goth, "the easier to mow." And the inequality of men is far more remarkable when we compare them as to their influence on future generations. The names of Joseph and of Daniel have outlived the glories of Egypt and of Babylon. The Infant of Bethlehem outweighs all the millions who were taxed by Cæsar Augustus.

One more point to be noted in the history before us is the atonement which David made for his fault. On the threshing-floor at which the destroying angel had stayed his hand, David not only offered sacrifice, but prepared to erect a house to the Lord as a manifest and enduring sign that God was the true King of Israel. Thus from that three days' pestilence there sprang the most illustrious building ever raised by human hands, and David's presumptuous sin was turned by God's grace, through his repentance, to a testimony for all time that holiness, not numbers, is the true glory of a nation.

We also, brethren, are called to a similar work, both as a people and as a Christian congregation. We have before us a task which may not unfitly be illustrated by that which employed the last years of David's reign. The purpose of our lives may be described as the preparing of a temple to the Lord our God, in which we are fellow-workers with Him. Of that spiritual Temple Christ is the corner-stone, the Apostles are pillars. The timber and the iron, the silver and the gold, are living Christian souls, redeemed from sin, and joined together in unity of spirit. This mortal state of ours is a period of preparation, for collecting and shaping the materials for the heavenly Temple. When Solomon built the Temple on Mount Zion, he found the preparation made beforehand. No sound of axe or hammer disturbed the sacred stillness of the place. Each piece was fitted exactly, so that they had only to be brought together.

"Like some tall palm, the noiseless fabric grew."

In these particulars we may trace a resemblance which is not merely fanciful, between the Temple of Jerusalem and the spiritual Temple of which it is the type. Here, in the labours and strife of the present world, our souls are being shaped for their future destination, and the question for each one at the last must be, "Are you prepared?" We know well how imperfectly as yet the several parts of the fabric of Christ's Church on earth fit together:

how faults of character, and the bias of prejudice which hinders conscientious men from uniting in Christian fellowship, mar the perfection of Christ's Church on earth. That building which was founded wonderfully on the day of Pentecost by the power of the Holy Spirit, is rent asunder by the earthquakes of human passion. But we look in faith and hope to a better life, when in heaven, if not on earth, the broken walls of Christendom shall be reunited.

Moreover, while we see in the New Jerusalem of St. John's vision the true fulfilment of the types of the city of David and the Temple of Solomon, it is not without reason that we look to the building of the Temple as an example and precedent for erecting houses dedicated to God's worship, and using therein all the means which we have received from Him, to make them worthy of His service. Within the last generation there has been a great and widespread revival of Church-building, which bears witness to a revival of religious devotion. Yet we cannot compare the best of modern edifices with the Cathedrals and Abbeys of the Middle Ages. Our work of this kind falls very far short of the work of our forefathers. Men are more numerous, money more abundant, engineering skill and resources more varied, and the pomp and pride of man are displayed in magnificent structures, both public and private. What is wanting is that solemn recognition of God's supreme majesty which David made, when his heart smote him for numbering his people. If we pass by Canterbury or York, or any of our ancient cathedral cities, we see the towers and spires of God's house far above the buildings of the neighbourhood. In a modern town we observe no such thing. The Town Hall, the Exchange, the Law Courts, the Railway Stations, the factory chimneys, are the objects which catch the eye. This would matter little, if we were well assured that God's presence was felt spiritually in the heart of our nation. The visible tokens of His presence might be spared, if His presence in spirit were duly recognized. But material prosperity has undermined our faith in that which is unseen and spiritual; and it is not without grave anxiety that we can look forward to the times which are coming upon us. Let it be our part, at all events, to cherish the lessons of Holy Scripture, and consider that which really belongs to our peace: not our numbers, nor our wealth, but our uprightness before God.

XVIII. SOLOMON.

"There shall not be any among the kings like unto thee all thy days."—1 *Kings* iii. 13.

(**Eighth Sunday after Trinity**, P.M.)

THE magnificence of Solomon's court is very fully described in the Bible, in the first book of Kings, and the second book of Chronicles. His reign was a course of uniform prosperity, and was therefore comparatively uneventful. Instead of struggles and adversities and dangers, such as accompany the troubled life of David, we have particulars of the splendid despotism with which Solomon ruled over Israel and over the nations around. The change in Jewish history is as when a river, which has been rushing violently over rocks, with waterfalls and eddies, widens to a broad stream in the midst of a fertile plain.

Solomon's reign was the golden age of Israel. Then, and then only, the Jewish kingdom held a conspicuous place among the empires of the East. Then Jews were free men, and Gentiles their servants. We read in 1 Kings iv. 20, "Judah and Israel were many, as the sand which is by the sea in multitude, eating and drinking and making merry." Their king's dominion extended from the great river of Assyria to the great river of Egypt. The fame of his wisdom and power lingered for centuries after his time in fantastic traditions: as for instance, what is often mentioned in the Arabian Nights, that his seal kept evil spirits in bondage. To the Jews themselves, in later ages of exile and subjection, the memory of "Solomon in all his glory" became more and more precious, shaping their hopes of the future reign of the Messiah, the second and greater Prince of Peace. And if we seek for a type of the kingdom of Christ, we can find none more suggestive to our imagination than that Holy City of Mount Zion, as it was in Solomon's reign, secure from all enemies, ruled with consummate wisdom, adorned outwardly with all the treasures of the earth, and inwardly with the beauty of holiness.

Jerusalem in Solomon's day was an object of reverential admiration as a holy place, to Jew and Gentile. From the utmost parts of the known world the choicest treasures were brought to enrich that high-built city among the mountains, which seemed, and still seems, to hold a central position in the midst of Europe, Asia, and Africa. At one port the ships were laden with beams of cedar for the royal palace and the Temple. At another they bore a still more costly freight of gold and ivory. Long trains of camels and horses were seen journeying from inland cities with tribute for the great King. As they approached the Holy Land, they found it still a land flowing with milk and honey, a land of rich pastures and flowery banks, not laid waste and barren, as travellers see it now. The city itself rose more steeply above the valleys at its base, encircled by hills which to the Psalmist's eye represented the care of the Lord for His people. We may imagine in their freshness the massive walls of stone, the gilded roofs reflecting the sun, the cloud of incense rising above the Temple, the vast concourse of the tribes of Israel, as they assembled to be present at the Feast of Dedication. Any pilgrim going forward with the crowd up the acclivity might see there the dazzling retinue of the King, the chariots, the horsemen, the body-guard of infantry with shields of beaten gold. Then, with hushed voices and beating hearts, the spectators might catch a glimpse of Solomon himself, "fairer than the children of men," impressing a sense of awe upon all who saw him by the majestic dignity of his presence. Supreme alike in temporal and in spiritual government, he made intercession before God in the name of his people, solemnly, upon his knees; and then, standing and turning to the multitude, he dismissed them with his blessing. In this union of visible splendour with the sacred privileges of his office, as guardian of the worship of the one true God, there is an exaltation which invests Solomon with a majesty beyond that of merely human sovereignty.

Moreover, they who were admitted to converse with him in his presence-chamber, found a new cause of wonder in the wisdom which flowed from his lips. Of all his manifold gifts his wisdom has contributed to his fame the most. It was this which he asked of God before all things; and it is this which is associated above all things with his name.

Yet if we look below the dazzling surface of Solomon's glory, we find much to qualify the admiration which it inspires at first. His wisdom was shortsighted, as to the welfare of his people, and as to his own happiness. His reign left a legacy of evil to his successor. The sumptuous works, which appeared so sure a sign of prosperity, were built by the enforced labour and contributions of oppressed subjects, who took the first opportunity to throw off the yoke. His brilliant qualities, and the activity of mind which took delight in every form of art and science, passed by degrees into jaded voluptuousness. The same king who had borne a priestly and prophetic office in the dedication of the Temple of the Lord Jehovah, brought idolatry back in his old age to the hills and valleys of the Holy Land. So the splendour of Solomon's reign was eventually tarnished; and when we survey his life on the whole from a distance, we are little disposed to approve it. Time brings out clearly the simple outline of the past, without its accessories; like sunset among the mountains, when the light fades from the purple heather of the hills, meadow and foliage become hidden in obscurity, and nothing is visible except the dark ridges against the sky. For us the glory of Solomon has faded. When we desire that we may die the death of the righteous, it is never of him that we think, nor do we pray that our last end may be like his.

A life so many-sided is full of spiritual instruction. In general it sets forth the lesson, that there is a flaw in the brightest and rarest gifts, if these gifts are not consecrated by an humble spirit. To illustrate fully this lesson in the case of Solomon, would be a subject too extensive for consideration at one time. But, without entering much into detail, we may profitably note a few main points.

1. As to Solomon's wisdom. It was a Divine gift, as it is to all who are endowed in any measure with a similar gift; but it is attended with special temptations. Our Lord charged His disciples to be "wise as serpents, and harmless as doves," implying that the wisdom of the serpent was apt, of itself, to be wanting in the quality of innocence: apt to go along with a character alienated from God and man, like that of the fallen angels. This dove-like innocence was certainly wanting in the character of Solomon. He lost that grace which is so exquisitely described in the Psalms—

> "I refrain my soul and keep it low,
> Like as a child that is weaned from his mother;
> Yea, my soul is even as a weaned child."

Solomon used his great powers to minister skilfully to his own grandeur and pleasure. The wisdom, which was given to him in answer to his high-minded prayer, became in his hands an instrument of tyranny. He understood how to make men subservient to himself, how to break the wills of the rebellious, how to employ their talents and industry to his own purposes, how to combine the resources of nature and art most effectively. But in all this his aim was selfish, at least in his later years.

2. As to his other varied gifts of heart and mind, we may observe that each turned off from the service of God and His people to mere self-gratification. The book Ecclesiastes gives us apparently the bitter fruits of his own experience; and its record is summed up in the words, "Vanity of vanities, all is vanity." No book that we can read gives us clearer evidence of the sinfulness of human nature, as common to mankind. We may indeed trace indications of the fall of man in all classes, civilized and savage. The most degraded show signs that they were made for a higher life; the most refined show the taint of ignoble pride and passion. What we have especially to learn from such experience as Solomon's, is the

insufficiency of culture as an antidote to sin. Solomon, endowed with everything within him and around him which could exalt and complete the present life, felt a void in his heart which the world could not satisfy; and, failing in his search for happiness, he stooped to baser pleasures, until he contaminated his soul by foul idolatries. In this respect he is a leader among many who, even to the present day, have exhibited the spectacle of a lofty mind in combination with a degraded soul. Only the grace of God in Christ can supply the principle of eternal life, without which the most brilliant gifts are vanity of vanities, their brightness the brightness, not of health but of consumption, a hectic glow which forebodes rapid decay.

3. As to Solomon's eminent work of piety in building the Temple, it was a work which he inherited from his father, and which had the express approval of God, by the mouth of the prophets and other manifest signs. We may therefore take it without hesitation for an example, and consider, that no pains and cost are too great to bestow upon the place which is consecrated for the worship of God. Christ's law imposes no express obligation in this matter, and affirms our spiritual freedom to

worship the Father acceptably, without any restriction as to places of worship. But Christ's law is far from disallowing consecrated places of worship. The Apostles, immediately after Christ's Ascension, were continually in the Temple; and, when the Temple was destroyed, the primitive Christians took the first possible opportunity, even before it was safe, to meet together for prayer and praise and Holy Communion in places especially set apart, which they adorned as much as they dared. The general experience of Christendom seems to show that sacred architecture and sacred music are helps to spiritual worship. Some there may be, who by temperament or by habit find most warmth of spirit within, when external appearances are cold and bare. But this disposition is not common, and probably is a reaction against the superstitious abuse of art. Most men, even if they dissent from the forms of our Church, feel the solemnity of such buildings as our grand cathedrals,

" Where through the long-drawn aisle and fretted vault,
The pealing anthem swells the note of praise."

Nevertheless there is danger that the art which twines itself round spiritual religion may, like a parasitical plant, choke the life of spiritual religion, and may be cultivated, not for God's sake, but for the art's own sake. So it proved in the case of Solomon. His lapse into idolatry must be regarded in connection with the rest of his life. It was no mere accident, no mere old man's weakness, but the natural consequence of his self-indulgence. When a man turns his mind to the externals of religious service, to the building or the music, not for love of God, but for love of display, he is already far on the way to idolatry. The pomp and fancy and vanity, which are gratified at one time by the erection of a world-renowned Temple to the Lord God of Israel, may at another time devise shrines for Baal and Ashtoreth. Doubtless in his earlier enthusiasm Solomon was incapable of such profanation. But self-love corrupts even the most sacred affections; and there is deep truth in the saying, that a way is open to hell even close beside the gates of heaven. The heathen wives who led Solomon astray were wives of his own choosing, brought to augment his royal state. Thus he became a tempter to himself. Morally, he cast himself down from the pinnacle of the Temple, in the presumptuous pride of life.

Any censure which we may pass on Solomon

should be uttered rather in warning for our own guidance, than in judgment of sins which we can hardly measure equitably. How the great Judge of all will deal at the last with those whom He has exposed to the temptations of power, riches, and genius, is hidden from us at present. We neither can define the strict rule of justice in such cases, nor yet the extenuating pleas of mercy. What we do see, in Solomon's case and others like his, is the spectacle of a grand life ruined. And the personal application of this example is, to resist the temptation to make a selfish use of our talents and opportunities, whatever they may be. Our solemn acts of worship will not keep us right, if in our worship we consult our own pleasure more than God's will.

To point this lesson more clearly, let us turn from the spectacle of Solomon in his glory, to that other Son of David, who was to fulfil what Solomon missed. The true Messiah, the Anointed Prophet, Priest, and King of Israel, came before men under circumstances which in some respects were a parallel to those of Solomon, in others a most impressive contrast. He came in wisdom and power to take the throne of His father David, but the spirit in which He came was a spirit of humility and self-devotion, as it is written, "Lo, I come to do Thy will, O God." Among the lessons which the history of Solomon conveys, none is more instructive than the absolute contrast which he presents, in his pride and selfishness, to the self-sacrifice of the Lord Jesus Christ. David's glowing descriptions in the Psalms of the reign of the royal son who was to come after him, might seem on the surface to be accomplished in Solomon; but the more we study his words, the more clearly a deeper and spiritual meaning unfolds itself. The Messianic prophecies were to be fulfilled, not with cedars of Lebanon and gold of Ophir, not with stately buildings and magnificence, but in the life of One who "came not to be ministered unto but to minister, and to give his life a ransom for many." The obedience of Christ, the humility of Christ, the love of Christ, are His titles to supreme reverence, that every knee should bow in His name. The Cross of Christ, the symbol of atoning self-sacrifice, is become an ensign of glory; while the reign of the selfish king is summed up in his own words, "Vanity of vanities; all is vanity."

XIX. JEROBOAM.

"This thing became a sin."—1 *Kings* xii. 30.

(Tenth Sunday after Trinity, A.M.)

OF the things which were written of old time for our learning, few are more instructive than the history of the disruption of the glorious realm of David and Solomon. To apply the lesson closely to modern times is hardly possible, without entering further than is convenient into the details of modern politics. But some great general principles are plainly to be inferred from this history; and of these, two are prominent. God approved the political division of Israel and Judah: "the cause was from the Lord." God disapproved the religious division of Israel and Judah: "this thing became a sin."

Solomon, Rehoboam, and Jeroboam are concerned in the matter, each bearing a distinct and important part. Solomon's idolatry in his old age drew upon him a prophetic warning.

"The Lord said unto Solomon, Forasmuch as this is done of thee, and thou hast not kept my covenant and my statutes, I will surely rend the kingdom from thee, and will give it unto thy servant." The first prompting of Jeroboam to revolt came from the prophet Ahijah. He was apparently engaged in his duties, without any rebellious design, when the rude hand of the prophet caught his new robe, tore it in twelve pieces, and gave ten of them to him with God's message, "Behold, I will give ten tribes to thee."

In this, as in so many other cases, God's will was accomplished by means of a chain of natural consequences. The costly establishments which Solomon provided for his heathen wives and their sumptuous worship increased the taxation of the kingdom. The people grew discontented; and at Rehoboam's accession they presented a formal remonstrance. "Thy father made our yoke grievous: now therefore make it lighter, and we will serve thee." The young king, taking counsel from companions of his own age, gave his people an insolent answer. A cry was raised, like that which had been heard in David's reign, "To your tents, O Israel." Ten tribes declared their independence of the house of David. Rehoboam assembled an army, but a prophet forbade him, in God's name, to go to war for this cause. So the kingdom is rent asunder, and that by God's express decree. The secession of the ten tribes was not a rebellion against the Lord God of Israel, but a fulfilment of His word already spoken. "The cause was from the Lord." God has not sanctioned the arrogant claim of kings to deal with their subjects as they please. He does not suffer them to act on their own will, without regarding His.

In the division of the kingdom, Ephraim, the tribe of Joseph and of Joshua, asserted its ancient claim of leadership against that of Judah. An Ephraimite, Jeroboam, was chosen for king. He is a type of a worldly-wise man. His valour and prudence were such, that even Solomon looked upon him with suspicion as a dangerous rival, and caused him to fly to Egypt for safety. Thence he was called back by the revolting tribes as the fittest man to lead them. Their choice is approved by the inspired voice of God's prophets. It was not Jeroboam's conduct in taking the crown of Israel, but his conduct in altering the religion of Israel, which earned for him the reproach by which he is known in Scripture, as "Jeroboam the son of Nebat, who made Israel to sin."

Powerful as was Jeroboam's kingdom, in comparison with the small remnant which was left to Rehoboam, the kingdom of Judah had the advantage in one respect. There was the sanctuary of the Lord at Jerusalem, to which the tribes went up to offer sacrifice. Jeroboam began to fear, not unreasonably, that the attraction of the Holy City would draw the hearts of his people from him. He forgot that he was God's minister, and began to think, as many other rulers have thought since his time, that nothing was so sacred as the maintenance of his own authority. Having to choose between religious duty and personal interest,—between the law which God had given to Israel and the confirmation of his own power, he chose the latter. He told the people that it was too much for them to go up to Jerusalem. He introduced a form of worship which he had learned in Egypt, the worship of the Calf, two golden images of which he erected, one in Dan, at the north of his kingdom, the other in Bethel, at the south.

His conduct has been compared to Aaron's, and has been excused, as a necessity of state policy, but it seems in truth to be without excuse. The unholy character of his device to attach to himself the people of Israel is shown by two facts: that the priesthood held aloof from him, and that he changed the seasons for his solemn festivals. He appointed priests who were not of the tribe of Levi: and he fixed, instead of the great feasts which celebrated God's mercies to Israel, a day of his own choosing, the fifteenth day of the eighth month. By a curious coincidence, it is the corresponding day in the modern calendar, August 15, which was chosen by Napoleon for an imperial holiday in France.

Thereupon the same Divine voice which had prompted and justified the rebellion of Jeroboam denounced his act of schism. A prophet was sent from Judah to rebuke him and curse his altar on the day of his feast of dedication. At the word of this prophet, who is called by tradition Iddo, the altar was blasted; and the king's arm stretched out against him was paralysed, until he interceded with God that it might be made whole again.

If the story had concluded at this point, it would have been an impressive warning against acts of religious division. But the lesson is made more emphatic, and richer in personal application, by the sequel of the story of the man of God from Judah. So far he had been discharging his public office; but he had also received a commission from God which was for himself privately: not to eat bread nor to drink water in that place, nor return by the same way. The meaning of this commission is not difficult to guess. It was doubtless to keep the man of God from the dangerous influence of social intercourse with his apostate brethren; and further, through him, to warn the children of Judah to separate themselves from the fellowship of the ten tribes, so long as they persisted in their idolatry.

The man of God refused Jeroboam's hospitality, and proceeded to go homeward, as he had been bidden, by another way: but he loitered on the road, and was overtaken by an old prophet of Bethel who went after him. This old man tried to seduce him from his obedience; not for ill-will, but for relief to his own mind. He was doubtless one who had taken part in Jeroboam's idolatry against his better judgment, and he sought to quiet his troubled conscience by making friends with the stranger who bore the Lord's message. It is a common thing for time-serving men to seek to ally themselves with men of stricter principles, and by social companionship to seem to be more virtuous than they really are.

The prophet of Judah was beguiled by the false pretensions of the prophet of Bethel. He had not the single eye which keeps the whole body full of light. He listened and returned. But at supper the lips of the prophet of Bethel were opened by Divine inspiration. He turned round upon his guest, and cried, "Forasmuch as thou hast disobeyed the mouth of the Lord, ... and hast eaten bread and drunk water in this place, of the which the Lord said to thee, Eat no bread and drink no water, thy carcase shall not come into the sepulchre of thy fathers." Accordingly the prophet of Judah was killed by a lion on his way home; and as a sign of the special working of God's providence, the lion did not eat the prophet's carcase, nor tear the ass on which he rode.

Every particular of this story carried its lesson of warning home to the people of Judah, deterring them from communion with the worshippers of the calves in Dan and Bethel. To the same effect St. Paul says to the Corinthians, "I write unto you not to keep company, if any man that is named a brother be a fornicator, or covetous, or an idolater, or a reviler, or a drunkard, or an extortioner; with such an one no not to eat." It is in this direction—namely, with reference to moral conduct—that we must look for the main application to Christ's kingdom of the story of the disobedient prophet. Let the true servants of Christ beware of intimate companionship with any whose lives are a scandal to their Christian profession.

Returning to the larger subject of which this story forms a part, the division of the kingdom, we can hardly fail to observe some interesting points of correspondence in our own national history, which have often exercised the minds of thoughtful men. Our fathers were provoked at the Reformation to cast off a foreign ecclesiastical yoke, which so far resembled the oppression of Solomon that it was outwardly magnificent and inwardly corrupt, tainted with idolatry, exacting, and burdensome. When the Church of England was declared independent of Rome, and the Papal supremacy was renounced, there was good reason as of old to say, "the cause was from the Lord." But the steps which followed in the Reformed Churches of Europe have in some cases imitated one or other of the faults of Jeroboam. As soon as extreme Reformers, like the English Puritans and the Scottish Presbyterians, not content with the spiritual liberty already won, strove to extirpate the ancient worship, root and branch, and to break the continuity of Holy Orders, "the thing became a sin." We are not in bondage to the usages of the early Church, but we ought not to divide ourselves from the fellowship of the early Church. It was no work of the Holy Spirit, but of an unholy spirit, to differ for the sake of difference, to reject the use of the Apostles' Creed, the primitive ordinance of laying on of hands, the sacred seasons of Christmas, Easter, and Whitsuntide, and others, the solemn dedication of Houses of God, the sign of the Cross, and many more such visible links which joined the present in a chain of fellowship with the past. Doubtless it might be said of many of these things that they had been perverted to superstition. But it may be answered no less truly, that the intemperate zeal of such Reformers has put weapons in the hands of the enemies of all religion, and sown the seeds of much unbelief which we have cause to deplore in the present day.

There may be also, on the other side, some

ground for the reproach of the Nonconformist sects against the Church of England, that our discipline has been too lax, that our liturgical forms have been too rigid, that we have suffered in spiritual vigour by unworthy subjection to the State. I cannot say that these reproaches are utterly without foundation; but the last half century has done much to diminish their force. On the whole, I think that the present state of the Church of England will bear comparison with that of any Christian society, great or small; and chiefly in its willingness to recognize faults, and amend them.

As it is, our position in Christendom is one of singular advantage and responsibility. We have by the grace of God combined the benefits of Evangelical Truth and Apostolic Order. On these principles, and on no others, can the divisions of the Church be healed. The largest section of the Christian world, that which adheres to Rome, has corrupted the simplicity of Evangelical Truth. Other sections, dividing and sub-dividing at their will, have lost sight of the primitive form of Apostolic Order. Between these two extremes there is no way of reconciliation except through the intervention of a Church such as ours, which holds fast with filial reverence the cardinal principles of both: Catholic in the true sense, being one with the Church of the Apostles, and also one at heart with those, all the world over, who love the Lord Jesus Christ in sincerity.

When we look from our island to the troubles of the Continent of Europe, we may well believe that a glorious future is before the Anglican Church, the prospect of being a guide to others, according to Zechariah's prophecy of the Jews (viii. 23): "In those days it shall come to pass that ten men shall take hold out of all languages of the nations, even shall take hold of the skirt of him that is a Jew, saying, We will go with you: for we have heard that God is with you of a truth."

In order that we may not be found unworthy of so high a charge, we must practise among ourselves the principles to which we testify in public. To be sound Churchmen, we must be first of all good Christians. The root of evil in schism is self-will, the opposition of our private choice to the authority set over us, or to the welfare of our brethren. This root springs up in every Christian society, alike in isolated congregations and in world-wide communities. But it is the work of the Spirit of Christ to subdue self-will, that His prayer may be fulfilled, "that they all may be one." If our profession of churchmanship is to be more than hypocrisy, it must bear fruit in meekness, fairness, patience, and charity. By fruits like these Christ's people are to be known.

XX. AHAB.

"How long halt ye between two opinions?"
1 *Kings*, xviii. 21.

(Eleventh Sunday after Trinity, A.M.)

THIS indignant question was uttered by the prophet Elijah on Mount Carmel, when he stood forth as the champion of the true God against the priests of Baal. It is one of the most impressive scenes in the Bible. We contemplate with admiration the grand figure of the prophet, steadfast amid a wavering multitude, alone to outward appearance, but not in spirit, for he knew that the eternal God was with him. Scripture contains only one more sublime instance of unfaltering trust, and that is the day of decision on Mount Calvary, a remarkable antitype. The Son of God stood in solitary protest against the world, because its deeds were evil.[1] Priest and people, Pilate and Herod, were set against Him; and His cause

[1] St. John, vii. 7.

was tried by a Sacrifice, the Sacrifice of Himself. From morning until evening the beholders were in suspense. But the heavens, which were cloudless over Carmel, were darkened over Calvary. There were mockers present, who took up the name of Elijah, saying, "He calleth for Elias; let us see whether Elias will come to save him." At the last, when He gave up the ghost, the centurion was moved to say "Truly this was the Son of God;" but we must look on to Pentecost for the completion of the analogy. Then, and not till then, fire came down from heaven at the descent of the Holy Spirit; and the miracle of that day was the founding of the Christian Church.

I wish to insist upon one point, which is conspicuous in the example of our blessed Lord, and also in that of Elijah, the value of steadfastness. In every age decision of character has a large part in the shaping of events. The world, like the people of Ahab's kingdom, is apt to halt between two opinions, doubting whether to worship Baal or Jehovah. So the later Jews cried one day "Hosanna," another day "Crucify." The issues of the world depend mainly on a few individual souls of constant purpose, who dare to resist the ebb and flow of the world's humours. This force of character is sometimes for good, as in Elijah, sometimes for evil, as in Jezebel.

King and people were subject to the rival influence of these two powerful souls. Ahab allowed his Sidonion queen to introduce her own religion into the land, and the people submitted. When Jezebel set up her altars on the hill-tops of Israel, when wizard prophets crowded the royal courts, and the prophets of the Lord took refuge in caverns from the slaughter of their brethren, the people were half-inclined to believe that Baal and Ashtoreth must be mighty gods, since they seemed to have the upper hand. It required a miracle to draw from them the confession, "Jehovah, He is the God! Jehovah, He is the God!"

The personal indecision of the king is more fully and instructively shown in the story of Naboth's vineyard. That most interesting and tragical story is eminently adapted to teach us the close connection between weakness of character and wickedness. In this affair Ahab appears a mere tool in the hands of his resolute wife. He desired to complete the symmetry of his palace garden, or Paradise, as it was called, by acquiring the adjacent piece of ground which belonged to Naboth, a sturdy citizen of Jezreel. He offered to Naboth a fair price, or a better vineyard elsewhere; but Naboth insisted on his rights. He prized the land as the inheritance of his fathers, and he seems to have resented the king's apostasy from the religion of the true God. "Jehovah forbid," he said, "that I should give the inheritance of my fathers unto thee." Thereupon the weak king took his disappointment to heart, laid him down on his bed, and refused food, like a fretful child. In this condition the queen finds him, and learns the cause of his grief. "Dost thou now govern the kingdom of Israel?" she asks with scorn; "Arise and eat bread, and let thine heart be merry. I will give thee the vineyard of Naboth the Jezreelite."

While he hesitates, "letting I dare not wait upon I would," she takes her decision. But she sets to work in a roundabout way for the fulfilment of her purpose. She writes to the chief men of the city in the king's name, and bids them proclaim a fast, as if for some public calamity. Doubtless there was a plausible excuse for a stated fast-day; it might be an invasion of the Syrians, or a failure of the harvest, which might lead men to enquire "What sin has brought this visitation upon us?" The proclaiming of a fast involved the calling of a solemn assembly : and the queen gave orders to set Naboth on high among the people. That is, he was to be elected president of the assembly on this occasion, if I understand her design rightly. She knew the disposition of the man, and calculated on his committing himself by rebellious language, when he uttered his mind freely on the causes of God's wrath against the nation. This appears from her secret instructions, which were that witnesses should be suborned to say, "Naboth blasphemed God and the king." Wicked as this device was, it has been repeated in our English history. At the period of the Reformation, certain persons obnoxious to the Court were bidden to preach at St. Paul's Cross on prescribed texts, and spies were sent to take down their words, in order to accuse them.

Naboth fell into the trap which was laid for him. It is easy to imagine how a devout and patriotic Jew would speak of Baal and of Jezebel, if he were called to preside over an assembly of his fellow-citizens on a national fast-day. Thus, with the help of unscrupulous witnesses and servile judges, the Queen was able to keep up a show of justice, in putting him to death for treason and blasphemy. Naboth was found guilty under forms of law, and his goods became forfeit in regular course to the king. So now Ahab has his wish fulfilled. That corner of ground, for want of which he could neither eat nor sleep, has come into his possession, by his wife's daring artifice. He rises at once, and sets off in his chariot to feast his eyes on the vineyard which he coveted so much. But the pleasure of his visit is marred immediately; for there, in the place of murdered Naboth, he encounters a messenger of God, whom he regards as his personal enemy, the prophet Elijah, sent to curse him and his wicked house.

Ahab, notwithstanding his moral infirmity, was a brave soldier, one who could face his enemies in battle with courage; but the spiritual terror which fastens on an evil conscience made him quail before the man of God. The awful shadow of judgment to come crosses his path, never to leave it. Indeed, at that very moment the avenger of blood was close behind him. Jehu was one of two captains in attendance upon Ahab, an observant spectator of this interview. Had Ahab turned to look behind him, he would have seen, just over his shoulder, the face of the future destroyer of his wife and all his sons. Jehu with his blood-thirsty eyes, waiting behind Ahab, is a true picture of that certain retribution, which sooner or later finds the sinner out.

Familiar as we are with this tale of sin and judgment, we can pass the more readily from its dreadful particulars to the general lesson which strikes home to our own conscience. It shows most distinctly the connexion between moral weakness and moral wickedness. No instance could better illustrate the consequences of a wavering mind, which halts "between two opinions," between right and wrong. Ahab's conduct bears throughout the stamp of human nature, and is a warning to every one of us. Although the murder of Naboth stands notorious among crimes, the motives and steps which led to it are not far from the range of common life. Power and opportunity make the difference between the guilt of Ahab, and that of men who have never brought reproach on their name. His sin was an unlawful wish, a covetous desire for his neighbour's land. He is not related to have taken any part in the plot by which his wish was gratified. Without overt act of his own, he was guilty in God's sight, because he consented to the crime.

Others, no doubt, have pined and craved as eagerly for something which could not be had by fair means, but they have had no one like Jezebel, to give effect to their desire, no obsequious servants like the elders of Jezreel, to carry out an evil deed to its conclusion.

> "It is the curse of kings to be attended
> By slaves that take their humours for a warrant."[1]

Crimes are sometimes committed alone, single-handed; but the darkest crimes are usually divided between several agents, each of whom screens his conscience by taking only a part of the responsibility. Thus Ahab might say that he never intended to possess himself by foul means of Naboth's vineyard. Jezebel might say that she cared only for her husband's happiness. The elders of Jezreel could plead the authority of the king's seal, under which they acted. Thus an infamous crime is composed of several steps or parts; and no one concerned feels the enormity of the deed until the guilty conscience of the doers is startled by God's displeasure, expressed by His minister. The

[1] Shakespeare, "King John."

words of Elijah laid bare, as by a lightning flash, the secret guilt of Ahab and Jezebel.

Consider this warning, brethren, and consider it especially with reference to that fault which is at the root of the whole, the indulgence of sinful wishes. If unholy desires present themselves to your mind, do not give them entertainment. Satan is not to be trifled with; and he knows well how to avail himself of the moral debility which offers no resistance to the first overtures of temptation. In yielding to a mere wish of the fancy, cherishing it in thought, and vaguely hoping that by good luck it may be gratified, you may be drawn onward to steps from which at first you would have recoiled: as when Hazael said, "Is thy servant a dog, that he should do this thing?"

Weak sinners fall under the dominion of stronger wills than their own. The strange power, which seducers to evil gain sometimes over men and women who become their victims, is rarely won over the innocent, but over foolish dreamers of pleasant day dreams, who allow their imagination to be fascinated, until they have no will to resist. They halt between two opinions, "I would, and would not." Terrible as the power of evil is, it is not the ruling force of the world. If we choose Christ for our Master outright, His spirit will arm us against the tempter. In is written, "Resist the devil, and he will flee from you: draw nigh to God, and he will draw nigh to you."

The example of Ahab warns us against the indulgence of all sorts of unlawful and inordinate wishes; but it applies more especially to the sin of covetousness; and this is one of the besetting sins of the world in the present day. The desire of more land, more money, more goods, is an insatiable craving which grows by what it feeds on, like the thirst of one who drinks sea-water. A covetous man fancies that his present wish, some small addition to his possessions, is all he wants; but in truth it is only precious till it is won. I think that a large part of the prevailing complaints of "bad trade," and "bad times," are mere covetousness. The idea of progress has taken such hold of men's minds, that they look to gaining more and more, and take no count of what they have gained. And thus, while every town in the country shows growing prosperity in new public buildings, new well-built suburbs, and increasing population, the voices of discontent make themselves heard continually. It is a matter for each of us to look to, in our own lives. Unless we learn to control our wishes, to subdue the desire of gain before it becomes a passion, we shall lay ourselves open to the subtle temptations which present themselves opportunely, to gain our end by dishonourable means.

Covetousness is a sin which works its own punishment in this life: for no one is so miserable as a man who never knows how to be satisfied. For this reason the name of "miser" is given to the avaricious, in whom the desire of hoarding has superseded all other desires. But the Apostle Paul condemns the sin of covetousness on higher ground, identifying it with idolatry. The unprincipled and intemperate desire of gain is a sort of religion, a worship of Mammon. And this is the alternative which chiefly divides the English nation at the present time with the worship of God. Our choice lies, not between Jehovah and Baal, so much as between Christ and Mammon, especially in commercial life. There is not a little halting between two opinions, for a good many hope to reconcile the two services. But Christ says emphatically, "Ye cannot serve God and Mammon." One must give way to the other. We can have no serious doubt which is properly the Master, and which the Servant. Only He who made us for Himself can give to our souls the rest which we need in this life : and Mammon has no part or lot in the life to come.

XXI. ELIJAH.

"He requested for himself that he might die; and said, It is enough; now, O Lord, take away my life; for I am not better than my fathers."—1 *Kings* xix. 4.

(𝔈𝔩𝔢𝔳𝔢𝔫𝔱𝔥 𝔖𝔲𝔫𝔡𝔞𝔶 𝔞𝔣𝔱𝔢𝔯 𝔗𝔯𝔦𝔫𝔦𝔱𝔶, P.M.)

THE man who stands almost alone, in the record of his exemption from the common lot of death, is likewise almost alone in his prayer for death. Elijah, whose effectual fervour in prayer was such that he is singled out for a special example in the New Testament, at whose prayer the famine came upon Israel, and afterwards was removed, prays for himself that he may die, and his wish is not granted to him. God in His wisdom overrules the desires of His servants, and while He hears prayer, grants that which is better than a fulfilment of the express thing which is asked for. He comforted Elijah by giving him instructions to prepare for his departure, so far as to anoint a successor. But the time of his departure was not yet come;

and when the time came, it was a wondrous manner of leaving the world which God had in store for him.

Elijah's prayer for death was a request made in weakness and sorrow. Such utterances of holy men are not the less instructive for being faulty in themselves. They bring the Bible nearer to our own deepest thoughts. If the saints were in all things raised above the level of human nature, we should be unaware of the earnest heartrending struggles through which they passed. Their errors and failings teach us that they were men of like passions with ourselves, and so we learn to regard their characters as examples of virtue which is not superhuman, but within the hope and aspiration of every child of God.

That Elijah's prayer for death was asked amiss, and contrary to God's will, we may conclude from several reasons. He is reproved immediately by God; bidden to arise and eat, told that he has work to do yet, and that he is not alone, as he thinks, but one of a host of seven thousand known to God, who have not bowed the knee to Baal. His ministry is prolonged for some years, until after the death of Ahab and his son Ahaziah. We may indeed affirm as a general rule, that it is wrong to ask to die. Although the tired soul, worn out by disappointment, care, and sorrow, would fain lie down and go to sleep for ever, this wish of nature is a wish to be resisted, not made the object of voluntary prayer. We should not willingly fall out from the ranks of God's army, but march steadfastly on, under the banner of the Cross. The desire of rest is only legitimate in those who can say like Elijah, "I have been very zealous for the Lord God," or like St. Paul, "I have fought a good fight, I have finished my course." And even for them God has work to do, beyond their own imagination.

If we look more closely into the circumstances of Elijah's despondency, we shall find much to cheer us when our hearts sink under the passing clouds of affliction. We may observe that such depression of spirit is no proof of God's disfavour, for Elijah was eminently favoured by God; no sign of a bad conscience or of a misspent life, for his conscience was clear and his life holy. From his example it would seem as if despondency like his were apt to befall the more noble sort of minds, as a discipline to prevent them from exalting themselves above measure.

Let us follow the steps of Elijah from that sublime moment on Mount Carmel, when fire descended from heaven at his prayer. Standing there before the multitude of Israel, a solitary champion for the Lord Jehovah, he had put the worshippers of Baal to confusion, and made the river Kishon run red with the blood of eight hundred of their prophets. Rarely, if ever, has mortal man occupied a position so majestic in its grandeur; not Moses, when he stretched out his rod over the Red Sea; not Daniel, when he interpreted the mysterious writing at Belshazzar's feast.

From this more than royal height he is brought down in a few hours to the common level of humanity. A woman threatens to take his life, and he flies. Queen Jezebel, with an audacity which rose with danger, scorns to smite him secretly, but sends a messenger to tell him that he shall die to-morrow. Some secret inspiration warns him not to resist, but to seek safety in flight. He has not God's thunderbolts at command, to call down when and how he pleases, but only at such times as God wills. So now he hastens away for his life, a homeless, friendless man, pursued by the vengeance of a powerful queen. Weary and hungry, he sits down to rest in the wilderness, and looks back in painful retrospect on his mission as a failure. Already the glorious scene upon Mount Carmel begins to fade away into the past. The prophet's labour seems to have been in vain. To what purpose had he borne witness to the Lord in signs and wonders? Has not the nation relapsed again into Baal-worship? It is not hard to understand how a servant of God, suddenly cast down from so great a victory, and for the moment appearing to have spent his strength for nought, should pray that he might die.

The manner in which God encouraged his soul is very instructive. First, He sustained his fainting body by miraculous food; for the mind is dejected when the body is suffering from exhaustion. Then He led him, far away from the scene of his cares and labours, to the ancient place in which the children of Israel had received the Law and the Covenant, the wilderness of Horeb. There God manifested Himself to him by a vision, wonderful in its nature, and wonderful also in its appropriateness.

"Behold, the Lord passed by, and a great and strong wind rent the mountains, and brake in pieces the rocks before the Lord, but the

Lord was not in the wind; and after the wind an earthquake; but the Lord was not in the earthquake; and after the earthquake a fire; but the Lord was not in the fire; and after the fire a still small voice."

Not in the whirlwind, or earthquake, or lightning flame, but in the still small voice which is heard by the inward ear of conscience, is God's true presence revealed. Thus Elijah was taught to think less of outward signs, such as that which had taken place on Carmel, and more of inward spiritual experience, which is known only to God and each several soul. Elijah thought himself the only faithful servant of the Lord; but there were seven thousand others to whom the same still voice of the Holy Spirit brought assurance that God was with them. We may affirm as a general truth the lesson, which was intimated to Elijah concerning his own time, that the progress of God's kingdom is in stillness and silence. Like the leaven of the parable, gradually fermenting the meal, like the seed springing up man knows not how, God is bringing the work of His Spirit to maturity, while man sees nothing but failure. The glory and humiliation of Elijah set before us, on a highly magnified scale, a picture of the vicissitudes which not a few of us have to undergo. Something of the same kind we trace in the history of most men. Public life is full of instances. Without referring to examples of kings discrowned, outcast statesmen and princes reduced to beggary, let us look at homelier cases. Who has not felt at certain moments of his life that he has more laid upon him than he can bear, that his heart is ready to break in the unequal struggle against powers too strong for him?

The nearest parallel to such a case as Elijah's is that of a man who gives up his whole energies of mind and body to a public cause, with sincere conviction that it is for God's glory, for right and truth, that he is striving. A preacher denouncing the religious indifference of the populace, appealing to the doctrine of Christ and His Apostles against the worship of the god of this world, or resisting the plea of religious equality, will sometimes be, like Elijah, as a voice crying in the wilderness. His neighbours will not hear him. He incurs only disappointment, reproach, and ridicule. God tries his patience by prolonged delay. His cause is just and will prosper in the end, but not yet; not by his hands, nor in his time. He must be content to sow for others to reap. Of this protracted waiting we have the most signal instance in the human ministry of the Son of God. He worked miracles, apparently in vain. One day it was said of him by the Pharisees in bitter jealousy, " Behold the world is gone after him." Yet a few days later the fickle populace have turned away from Him, like an ebbing tide, and He is left alone to bear witness before Pilate of a heavenly kingdom, of which He was the divinely anointed King: King, without one single subject to confess Him openly on that day, except the poor crucified robber who hung beside Him. The apparent failure of Christ's mission to the eyes of the world, until the fires descended from Heaven on the Day of Pentecost, is an example and encouragement to all who labour in the cause of truth. It holds good for the ministers of Christ, for those who preach His Word in the Church, for those who serve Him by their writings or by their personal influence. A remarkable case in our own time is the work of the late Bishop of New Zealand, a work in its beginning successful and prosperous beyond most, but nevertheless overcast afterwards by reverses, which demanded strong faith to surmount them. The New Zealand Christians, alarmed at the encroachment of colonists from Britain, gave ear to the voices of false prophets of their own nation, who bade them reject the doctrine and the morality of the Gospel, and go back to their old fierce heathendom, the worship of devils, and feasting on human flesh. During this terrible outbreak Bishop Selwyn patiently watched over "the remnant that was left." How deeply he felt the apostasy of his flock, and how earnestly his faith wrestled with adversity, was shown long afterwards, when he lay on his death-bed. His mind wandered unconsciously from England to his southern diocese, over the space of many years, and he murmured in his last hours, "They will all come back: they will all come back."

Temporary failure there may be in the best of causes, with the best of instruments. But final failure in the cause of the Almighty and Eternal God there cannot be. Every righteous deed done in faith, and every true word spoken, is contributing visibly or else invisibly to the establishment of the kingdom of Christ for ever and ever.

Men of the highest aims and the noblest character are best able to feel sympathy with

Elijah in his hour of despondency. His weakness was of a kind which is felt most keenly by strong men, whose human powers are overstrained in a task which is beyond them. But there is another point of view, less closely analogous, but more popular, in which any one of us may feel his case to be like our own.

You must have felt sometimes, if not often, that you had an object in life more precious than life itself. If our minds dwell intently upon the gratification of a desire, whether the particular object of desire be worthy or unworthy, disappointment appears for a while to be like death, or worse than death. Disappointed ambition, disappointed love, and even disappointed avarice, take hold of the soul so firmly that they seem to draw the happiness of life with them, and leave nothing behind worth living for. Few have their desires and affections so well governed as never to despair under the loss of what is dearest to them; and few, it may be hoped, are so cold-blooded as to escape suffering by mere insensibility. By far the larger number of us value life, not simply for the animal pleasure of living, but partly as a means to some object in the future, which hope sets before us in rainbow colours. How often are such hopes disappointed! How rarely does any good in possession fulfil the anticipation of it! And yet, when earnest hope and expectation, stretched to the utmost, are suddenly snapped, the whole world seems to have nothing to offer to compensate the loss. Thus the perverse prophet Jonah wished to die, merely because God showed mercy to Nineveh, after he had foretold its destruction, and while he waited to see his prediction fulfilled.

Under all the disappointments and troubles which make life burdensome we need to see deeper and to see further. We need to open our eyes to the secret springs of comfort which God has, above what we can ask or think. And since we cannot without special revelation trace the working of God's mysterious purpose to distant ends, we must live more by faith, trusting in that which we do not see. Believe, brethren, that while you seek God's kingdom you have others by thousands like minded with you, though you have no personal knowledge of them. Believe also that if you fail in your own day, your life is not therefore a failure, but a preparation for others to build upon with success. Elijah anointing Elisha, and anointing Jehu and Hazael by Elisha's means afterwards, is a type of many more of God's chosen servants in every age, who bear adversity in their own generation, that God's cause may prosper in other hands, and are recognized long afterwards in their true place. Thus we read in the prayer of Moses, himself an instance of the same Divine law, "Shew thy servants thy work, and their children thy glory."

Our Lord Jesus Christ spoke to His disciples to the same effect: "One soweth and another reapeth." And by faith in Him and His eternal kingdom we are assured that hereafter, in the perfected communion of saints, "he that soweth and he that reapeth shall rejoice together." As Elijah and Moses were brought by the Spirit from heaven, to bear witness to Christ on the Mount of Transfiguration, we shall by the same Spirit be witnesses of His final triumph over death and sin, if we employ our lives in His service, looking forward with hope to the end, but without impatient desire to lay our burdens down. We, too, like Elijah, are sustained by heavenly food in the wilderness of life's journey. Not angels, but Christ Himself, feeds us with the manna of His precious Body and Blood, that our life may draw strength from His life.

XXII. MICAIAH.

"I hate him, for he doth not prophesy good concerning me, but evil."—1 *Kings* xxii. 8.

(𝕮𝖜𝖊𝖑𝖋𝖙𝖍 𝕾𝖚𝖓𝖉𝖆𝖞 𝖆𝖋𝖙𝖊𝖗 𝕮𝖗𝖎𝖓𝖎𝖙𝖞, A.M.)

FEW men would dare to speak out shamelessly that which is here said by King Ahab. But the feeling is only too common. We are all more or less apt to judge others according to their judgment of us. We may therefore meditate profitably on this text, although it be the saying of a bad man. The lesson which it suggests combines with other passages in the same story, to show the power of conscience, as a witness on God's behalf against a rebellious will. Ahab King of Israel, and Jehoshaphat King of Judah, were about to make war with the Syrians. At the request of Jehoshaphat, Ahab summoned four hundred prophets and asked their counsel, as to the proposed expedition. The two kings sat in the palace gate of Samaria, not simply in their robes, as our version has it, but in armour,[1] while the courtly prophets foretold success to them. Something, however, troubled the mind of Jehoshaphat. He had apparently some scruples of conscience as to his alliance with Ahab; and the voices of the prophets did not altogether reassure him, though they professed to speak in the name of the Lord Jehovah. Perhaps he had heard of a stern prophet, Micaiah, who was not among them. So he asked, "Is there not a prophet of the Lord besides?" To this question Ahab made answer, "There is yet one man, Micaiah the son of Imlah, by whom we may enquire of the Lord; but I hate him, for he doth not prophesy good concerning me, but evil."

To satisfy his ally, Ahab sends for Micaiah, whom he had imprisoned, and the messenger urges him on the way to "speak that which is good," as the others had done. His answer was, that he must speak what the Lord said to him. Micaiah was evidently a prophet of the school of Elijah, one who did not fear to stand alone on God's side. The other prophets were time-serving men, who spoke as the king wished.

---

[1] Ewald, III. 500.

Among them probably were some of the same class with those who had contended with Elijah on Mount Carmel. There may have been others who had fallen away in the persecution of Jezebel. Troubled times like those were likely to produce a brood of apostates, men who were prophets of Baal when Baal was worshipped, and ready to speak in the name of Jehovah when their masters bade them, shifting to and fro in their religion, and constant only to their place at the royal table. Whoever they might have been, something in their face, or voice, or manner, betrayed them; and to the ear of Jehoshaphat there was a false ring in their eager predictions of success.

Micaiah's first words to the two kings are an echo of the words of the rest, "Go and prosper." But the tone of his voice showed that he was speaking ironically, as when Elijah had mocked the priests of Baal by saying, "Cry aloud, for he is a god." Ahab saw at once that Micaiah was mocking, and adjured him angrily to say nothing but the truth. Thereupon the prophet declared the vision which he had seen, of Israel scattered upon the hills as sheep without a shepherd. And he added a more mysterious vision, of the Lord sitting on his throne, surrounded by the heavenly host, and giving leave to a lying spirit to persuade Ahab to his destruction, by the mouth of false prophets.

This vision of Micaiah's leads us so deep into the hidden ways of God's providence, that we may well pause to reflect upon it. Hard as it is to understand, it reveals a Divine law which is no less certain than terrible. One of the judgments by which God visits upon wicked men their wickedness, is by blinding their eyes, and hardening their hearts. Thus St. Paul writes (2 Thess. ii. 11), "God shall send them strong delusion, that they should believe a lie;" and again, Romans i. 28, "As they did not like to retain God in their knowledge, God gave them over to a reprobate mind." But the passage which is most to the purpose is in the fourteenth chapter of Ezekiel, v. 7, 9. "Every one which . . . . . separateth himself from me, and setteth up his idols in his heart, ... and cometh to a prophet to enquire of him concerning me, I the Lord will . . . . . set my face against that man . . . . . And if the prophet be deceived, I the Lord have deceived that prophet." To be answered according to our idols, that is, to have our wishes granted to us to our sorrow, is the retribution with which

God visits us when our souls revolt from Him. So it was said of the children of Israel in the wilderness,

> "He gave them their heart's desire:
> And sent leanness into their souls."

So Balaam, rebelling at heart against the word of the Lord, was told to go his own way for a punishment. In the case before us, Ahab had long gone astray from God, and had hardened his heart by giving sanction to his wife's idolatry and overbearing tyranny. He now consults the prophets on a project on which his heart is set, and he receives from them an answer according to his wishes, not according to truth.

I believe, brethren, that these examples teach us a general rule of God's government, and one which concerns us nearly. If we fix our affections on objects of our own choice, and then pray to God, not according to the Lord's prayer, "Thy will be done," but according to the idol of our fancy, "My will be done," we are in danger of being punished by granting our prayer. They who shut their eyes to the truth lose the power of seeing truth, as creatures which live in dark caverns lose the faculty of sight. When self-willed men read the Bible, not humbly, but seeking a confirmation of their prejudices, they find what they want, and nothing else. Partisans are never at a loss for texts in favour of their party against their adversaries. To their eyes the Bible seems to say, "Go up and prosper." Meanwhile their adversaries have another string of texts, which the more skilful among them can draw out convincingly. "See here, and here, and here:" they say. How then are we to decide between opposing parties, each supported by an impressive show of Scriptural authority? It seems impossible; but one step is taken towards the knowledge of truth, when we resolve at all costs to seek the truth. By desiring to know the truth, we put ourselves at once out of Satan's hands into the hands of our heavenly Father. Even Ahab, depraved as he was, and willing to be deceived, had no sooner shown a desire to be told plainly what was true, than he had revealed to him the counsels of God in heaven.

The revelation did not stay him from his enterprise against the Syrians. He chose to treat it as a fiction of Micaiah's, and sent him back to prison. Yet he took the poor precaution of disguising himself when he went into battle. Not by such means was God's judgment to be eluded. An arrow shot at random (from the hand of Naaman, as men believed afterwards), found a crevice between the joints of his armour, and wounded him mortally. Then began to be fulfilled the terrible curse which Elijah had pronounced upon Ahab and his house. The life-blood flowed from his chariot into the street of Samaria, and the dogs licked it up. Jehoshaphat escaped in safety, but not without rebuke: for the prophet Jehu, son of Hanani, told him that the wrath of God was upon him for consorting with the ungodly.

Throughout this history we see, in various forms, the power which conscience exercises on men, whether they will or no. Jehoshaphat felt that he was doing wrong in allying himself with the wicked King of Israel. His conscience was uneasy; therefore he insisted on the prophets being consulted, and though four hundred agreed together in predicting success, he was dissatisfied until Micaiah was brought from prison and consulted with the rest. It is a surprising inconsistency that he persisted after all in the expedition, notwithstanding the warning of the prophet to whose word he had attached so much value. Yet inconsistency of this kind is often found in human nature. People take enormous pains to seek for advice, which they will not follow when they have it, if their minds are set upon another course. They pacify their conscience by asking counsel, and forget that it is not on this, but on their own conduct, that the issue depends.

Ahab likewise was troubled in conscience over this matter of the expedition to Ramoth Gilead. He was certainly not what is called a conscientious man, yet there was in his heart that inward monitor by which the Spirit of God pleads with men who are not utterly irreclaimable. In the words of a modern poem, "A little grain of conscience made him sour." He hated Micaiah the more, because Micaiah's predictions corresponded to the misgivings of his own soul. He felt that God spoke by him. The one faithful prophet was of more account than the four hundred prophets who were ready to speak smooth things. So it is related in the history of Florence that, when the great Lorenzo was on his death-bed, surrounded by friends and flatterers, he sent to the austere friar who had persistently denounced his manner of life, and asked him how to make his peace with God. Again in Ahab's case, as in Jehoshaphat's, the voice of conscience was ineffectual. It taught him to know what was right, but his will refused to bend to the knowledge. He sent the prophet of the Lord back to "bread of affliction and water of affliction," and went his own way, to his death.

To each of us, brethren, is given the power of conscience, which is illustrated in this history, and it is all-important for our spiritual welfare that it be not given to us in vain. In the doubts and difficulties of this life our conscience points steadfastly to God, as the compass points to the north. Like all human faculties it is imperfect, and needs adjustment by study of God's holy Word, as compasses need adjustment to make them exactly true. But in the meantime, until our conscience itself has been set by the light of revealed Truth, it is a practical monitor to us, always at hand, always faithful to the best knowledge we have, guiding us to what we should do, and what we should leave undone.

Fallen creatures as we are, there is in us a certain remnant of the Divine image in which we were created, a certain faculty which responds to the voice of God, recognizing it for His. We may imagine that if a child had been taken early from his native land, and brought up among foreigners, learning their language and forgetting his own, the sound of his native tongue once more would catch his ear, and arouse deep emotions in his heart. So there is in our conscience a Divine element, which seems, as it were, to hear its own language spoken in words which are uttered according to God's will. In matters of worldly fashion and custom, there is often a multitude on one side, and on the other perhaps no more than a single voice. Yet we feel in our inmost heart that the single voice is on God's side, and the multitude against Him.

There remains, after all, the practical decision, to follow the dictates of our conscience. Satan tempts us to stifle its voice, and draws off our thoughts to indignation against the true monitor: "I hate him, for he does not speak good concerning me, but evil." Those who seek advice, whether of God's minister or of any private friend, or otherwise, are ready to profess that they want only to hear the truth. But when the word is spoken contrary to their wishes, and wounding to their self-esteem, it is taken as a personal injury, and resented accordingly. A common artifice of the Tempter is, to point out some blemish in the character of one whose advice is disagreeable. If your friend becomes too strict for your habits of self-indulgence, you find that he has faults which you did not observe before. If your elders oppose your will, you discover that their judgment is not so infallible as you formerly supposed. You may be so far right, for no one is faultless. Nevertheless, your friends, with all their faults, are giving good counsel, and in rejecting them you are rejecting God, at the suggestion of an evil spirit.

Or again you may veil the spirit of hatred under the milder name of dislike, shunning those who seem to disapprove of your conduct, and taking for companions only those who are like-minded with yourself, or so easy as to wink at your favourite interests, whatever they may be. For one who will treat an unwelcome adviser as an enemy, there are scores who will quietly drop him, under plausible excuses, and lull to sleep the stifled cries of conscience. A few there are so ill-conditioned, that they resent not only good advice, but good example. Holiness is an offence to the impure: truth to the false: soberness to the intemperate. So by degrees the sense of right and wrong in our conscience may be perverted by neglect. A man who has fallen into a habit of wrong-doing, will sometimes think himself injured by the mere example of another who refuses to act like him.

While we live in this mortal state, the rebellion of our will against our better knowledge is the chief trial of us all. The body of sin is not destroyed in us, though by the grace of God we have begun a new and better life in Christ. The growth of our regenerate human nature, begun in Baptism, remains to be perfected through many years of spiritual discipline. We must endeavour, day by day, to live according to the light that is given to us. We must constantly and earnestly seek the grace of God's Holy Spirit, by prayer, and by means of that blessed Sacrament which Christ ordained for the strengthening and refreshing of our souls. Moreover, since prayer may become mechanical, we must watch, to keep our spiritual life awake. The flesh, which is weak in its aid to a willing spirit, is yet fearfully strong in resisting a spirit which is faint.

XXIII. NAAMAN.

"His flesh came again like the flesh of a little child, and he was clean."—2 *Kings* v. 14.

(𝔗𝔥𝔦𝔯𝔱𝔢𝔢𝔫𝔱𝔥 𝔖𝔲𝔫𝔡𝔞𝔶 𝔞𝔣𝔱𝔢𝔯 𝔗𝔯𝔦𝔫𝔦𝔱𝔶, A.M.)

COMPARED with other books, the Bible is remarkable for the notice which it takes of disease. Men prefer in general to forget the unwelcome truth that human nature is subject to a host of maladies, some acutely painful, others loathsome and revolting. While the details of crime are often studied with eager interest, the details of illness are more commonly put out of sight. Our attention is called in the Bible to the facts of disease for two reasons: first, that we may keep in mind the frailty of our nature; secondly, that we may have sympathy with the sufferings of our brethren. In the Old Testament we are taught to regard sickness, more particularly in the former of these two aspects, as a lesson of human frailty. Disease is shown to be a chastisement for sin, as in the plagues of Egypt, or a figurative symbol of sin, as in the ordinances of the Mosaic law. In the New Testament, on the other hand, we read of sickness chiefly in connection with acts of mercy for its relief. The life of our blessed Lord resembled that of a physician, so much did the healing of the sick divide His time with the preaching of the Gospel. He completed the lesson of the Old Testament by manifesting Himself as a giver of health alike to body and soul.

We have in some respects an anticipation of the miracles of the New Testament in the works of healing which are recorded of the prophet Elisha. The character of this great prophet is less clearly delineated in Holy Scripture than that of Elijah, whose mantle he received. But we may note many instructive features: his persistence in following his master to the end; his inspired power of insight and foresight; his generous magnanimity; his terrible flashes of indignation. Several of these traits come before us in the story of the healing of Naaman.

The Syrian general Naaman, whose miraculous cure is related in 2 Kings v., was suffering from some form of leprosy. It appears that the Jews classed under this name various kinds of eruptive disorders, and Naaman's does not seem to have banished him from human society, like the lepers of whom we read in the Gospels. Nevertheless, his lot was one of those strange contrasts which warn us how vain are the most coveted favours of God, without His ordinary gift of good health. Naaman was high in honour as a successful warrior. The king of Syria had been accustomed to lean upon his arm when he went to worship in the temple of his god Rimmon. His home was in the delightful city of Damascus, which was accounted an earthly Paradise. He had all that man's heart desires; "but he was a leper." Thus one stroke of God's hand turns all the bliss of life to heaviness. What are military glory, royal favour, riches, and luxury to a leper?

Among the servants of Naaman was a little Jewish maiden, taken captive in one of the Syrian invasions of the land of Israel. She spoke to her mistress of the great prophet Elisha, and wished that her master had an opportunity of being healed by him. It is an example worth noting of the service which may be rendered by kindly thoughtfulness in a humble station. Servants who wish well to their masters may be the means of giving help out of proportion to their own strength, like the mouse in the fable, gnawing asunder the lion's net. Even for children there is a ministry, within the proper range of their faculties, if they make the best use of them.

The words of the little slave-girl were repeated, and Naaman thought it worth his while to make trial of the prophet of Samaria. He set forth with chariots and horses to the King of Israel, bringing a somewhat peremptory letter of introduction from his master, the King of Syria.

It was evidently not without a haughty feeling of condescension that Naaman came to the door of Elisha's house, and his proud spirit broke out in anger when the prophet sent a message by a servant, instead of meeting him respectfully. He was hardly persuaded by his attendants to bathe in Jordan seven times, as the prophet bade him. "Are not the rivers of Damascus better than all the waters of Israel?" he said. Nevertheless, he obeyed the prophet's word, and he came forth from the river healed, his flesh as whole as that of a little child. Then his heart overflowed in gratitude to the prophet. He offered presents, which Elisha refused to accept; and he declared his resolution to worship no other god but the Lord Jehovah.

This miracle was one of the signs put forth, from time to time, to keep alive among the Gentiles a reverence for the God of Israel, although Naaman was not required to protest against the worship of Rimmon. The time was not yet come, by many centuries, when the God of the Jews was to be proclaimed as God of the Gentiles also, and true believers were to be martyrs for the faith, dying horrible deaths rather than offer incense on the altars of heathen gods. Not until the Holy Spirit descended on the Church, according to Joel's prophecy, were believers in the true God qualified to bear the good tidings of His kingdom for the conversion of the nations.

For us the story of Naaman has several applications, familiar and even homely, but well deserving of attention. There are times when the pride of reason is unwilling, like Naaman, to submit to a command which requires of us obedient submission to God's minister. In childhood we gain intelligence enough, to think we can understand those matters which concern our bodily and spiritual health, long before we can really understand them. The faculty of reason is developed much earlier than the faculty of right reason; and thus a clever youth learns to argue plausibly in support of his own wishes, although he is far from having a discernment of right and wrong. There is also, in young and old, the dead weight of prejudice, resisting a command to do some new thing, to which we have not been accustomed, and for which we see no good cause.

In its most literal sense, the precept of Elisha to Naaman, "Wash and be clean," is applicable to our day, as a means of bodily health. The healing of Naaman's leprosy was a miracle indeed; but miracles are commonly startling illustrations of the general laws by which God rules the world. We have learned of late years that infectious disorders of all kinds are averted in great measure by cleanly habits. That scourge of mankind, small-pox, which in its loathsome aspect is not unlike leprosy, takes the strongest hold of families which in their persons and their dwellings have neglected the plain rule to "Wash and be clean." The same may be said of typhus and cholera. When the dreaded visitation of sickness comes, men appeal to God for help, with prayers which seem often to be of no avail. Neither prayer nor medical skill can stay the pestilence, for a time at least. Yet if they had listened to the voice of God's minister, and the physician in these things is His minister, they might have prevented that which they cannot cure. Prayer is a spiritual force which works wonders, according to God's will; but in circumstances of this kind He requires deeds rather than words. Obedience to His laws of health is the most acceptable sacrifice.

Habits of body are also subtly connected with habits of mind. The slothful disposition, which neglects due care of the body, is apt to show itself in a want of mental discipline. Cleanliness, it has been wisely said, is near to godliness. For it is the outward symbol of a soul full of energy, abhorring that which is evil, and cleaving to that which is good. Hence the care of the body is a part, and not an unimportant part, in the training of children. In every age there will be hypocrites, who take the outside show instead of the reality, after the manner of the Jewish Pharisees. Thus we meet sometimes with mock refinement and mock purity. But the existence of the counterfeit, in this, as in other cases, serves to prove the value of that which is genuine.

Passing to the more spiritual lessons of Naaman's healing, we see in leprosy a type of sin, and in the words "Wash and be clean," a counterpart of the Gospel message, "Repent, and be baptized every one of you in the name of Jesus Christ for the remission of sins." These are the words of the Apostle Peter to the conscience-stricken multitude at Pentecost, when they asked, "Men and brethren, what shall we do?" Often has the pride of human reason rebelled against this message, as the pride of Naaman rebelled against the command to bathe in Jordan. Men ask incredulously, "What can the sprinkling of a few drops of water on the forehead do for the soul?"

It is not given us to understand the process by which the soul and body are connected, but we know they are connected together; and the sprinkling of water derives from God's ordinance a virtue which is not residing in itself, as a means of communication between Christ's kingdom and the soul of the baptized. The waters of Jordan were not intrinsically superior to the waters of Damascus. Both alike flowed from the snows of Lebanon. But Naaman, bathing in obedience to the word of God's minister, derived a benefit from Jordan which he could not have gained from the others.

So it may be said concerning the Apostolic ordinance of Confirmation. The pride of reason asks, "What is there in the laying on of hands?" Thus the rite of Confirmation is sometimes treated as if the candidate's act of self-surrender to Christ were the whole; and the Bishop's blessing is ignored. But let us consider both together. Suppose that the head bowed to receive the blessing is the head of a young Christian in the act of renewing the Covenant of Baptism; and that the hands extended to confer the blessing are hands of a chief pastor of Christ's flock, who has received his authority by personal succession from the Apostles of the Lord Jesus Christ. The laying on of hands in such cases has a palpable significance, which makes it easy to follow the teaching of the early Fathers of the Church, who regarded Confirmation as an act of spiritual strengthening, by the grace of the Holy Spirit.

Again, in the Lord's Supper, He has given His blessing to the ordinary food of the body, as means for the sustaining of the life of the soul. When we come to the Lord's Supper in reverent faith, and thankful memory of His atonement, we take home with us not only that which we brought, the same reverent faith, the same thankful memory, but a spiritual benefit over and above these, a grace which we could not have brought, the grace of communion with Him Who is our life and our salvation.

Thus, as a general rule throughout the whole system of the kingdom of Christ on earth, spiritual health and strength are conveyed by means which are in themselves utterly insufficient. By God's ordinance material channels serve to connect the faithful soul and the eternal Spirit of God. To think this impossible shows not only want of faith, but dulness of intelligence, for even physical facts throw light on the possibility. When we see how the mere contact of a wire completes an electric chain by which the people of two hemispheres communicate their thoughts, we can believe, if we have not proved by inward experience, that God's Spirit acts on the spirit of man by material channels, according to His omnipotent will.

Besides these lessons, which are suggested by the healing of Naaman, we have to consider one which belongs to the case of Gehazi. On him, as you will remember, fell the same hideous affliction of leprosy from which Naaman had been delivered. To him it availed nothing that he lived in the neighbourhood of Jordan's health-giving waters. He had been made partaker of heavenly gifts, which he had wilfully cast away. Living under the very eye of the Lord's prophet, and being thus daily reminded of God's law, he stooped to fraud in order to gratify his covetousness. What a downfall this was, we realize more vividly if we remember that Gehazi was to Elisha what Elisha had been to Elijah. But, instead of the prophet's mantle falling upon him, there fell on him the leprosy of Naaman.

Bear this in mind, brethren, if ever you find yourselves looking down on those who have been less favoured by God than yourselves. You have a just sense of your privileges as members of Christ, children of God, inheritors of the kingdom of heaven. You have become regenerate in the sacred waters of the New Covenant, you have been nourished on the spiritual milk of God's word, on the spiritual meat and drink of His sacraments. Yet "let him that thinketh he standeth, take heed lest he fall." The sins of Gehazi, covetousness and falsehood, are all the more deadly when they lurk under a sacred profession. There is a leprosy of spiritual decay which clings to apostate children of grace, and cannot by any means be healed; not even by the means which bring unregenerate souls to salvation.

XXIV. JEZEBEL.

"When Jehu was come to Jezreel, Jezebel heard of it: and she painted her face, and tired her head, and looked out of a window."—2 *Kings* ix. 30.

(*Fourteenth Sunday after Trinity*, A.M.)

SOME scenes in the Bible are described so dramatically, that we could almost fancy we had been present at them; and pictures, however skilful, fall short of the image which the Scriptures have already impressed upon our minds. Such is the advance of Jehu, when he came in fulfilment of prophecy as a minister of Divine vengeance on the house of Ahab. We seem to be eye-witnesses of his progress, as he hastens to his congenial task. Each detail which would fix the attention of a spectator is brought to our mind's eye. We see him raising a great cloud of dust with the furious speed of his chariot: we watch the messengers one after another, as they go to meet him, and fall back into the train of his followers: we see the two kings intimidated by his audacious front, and turning to fly: the arrow of Jehu drawn to the head, and presently quivering between the shoulders of the King of Israel. Last of all we see her who had been the ruling spirit of that age, the great Sidonian queen Jezebel, fading in beauty, but unfading in courage, as she faces the slayer of her son with the taunt, "Had Zimri peace, who slew his master?"[1] A desperate act of defiance; for the next moment she was cast under the horses' feet, and her corpse was devoured by dogs before nightfall.

Our distinct impression of these events makes them all the fitter to point a spiritual lesson. Jezebel was the representative of a religion which has had its votaries in every age, the religion of the god of this world. Those powers which a Christian renounces at his baptism, the world, the flesh, and the devil, were as gods to the Phœnician race from which Jezebel sprang. The worship of Baal, which Jezebel introduced, and against which Elijah strove in the name of the Lord Jehovah, was a religion which consecrated the baser passions of human nature. In later times, when the natives of Tyre and

[1] Or, "Is it peace, thou Zimri, thy master's murderer?" (*Revised Version.*)

Sidon had migrated westward, the same religion was conveyed to Greece, and took a hundred varied forms of idolatry. Then Greek art captivated Rome, and through Rome the whole modern world. Thus the old conflict on Mount Carmel, between the prophets of Baal and the prophet of Jehovah, is renewed whenever art, and fashion, and luxury, are exalted into a rule of life in opposition to the moral law of the Eternal God.

It is not by chance, but with remarkable consistency, that Jezebel is presented before us in the text with her face painted and her hair tired. The original is more minute: for it describes her eyelids as dyed with antimony, which was used to make the eyes look bright and large. Arts of this kind are thoroughly in harmony with idolatrous worship. Vanity and falsehood in personal adornment are of a piece with the vanity and falsehood in religion, of which Jezebel is the most notable representative. In the kingdom of this world, as in the kingdom of heaven, there are outward and visible signs to which certain inward and spiritual realities correspond. Satan has what may be called his sacraments, which symbolize influences on the soul which are contrary to God's grace. The world recognizes such fashions as the painted eyes of Jezebel, for symbols of a worldly mind.

If these and similar fashions become prevalent in a Christian land, it is a token of a pagan reaction, in which the multitude bow down the knee to Baal, possibly without knowing what they do.

We shall do wisely to consider, with more care than is usual, how far it is right for the servants of Christ to follow the world's train in changes of the fashion of dress. We have had much cause of late years to reflect upon this question, for the cost and style of dress has been a frequent topic of conversation as being extravagant. In current popular literature of all kinds it is discussed, mostly with disapproval, as the characteristic of a self-indulgent age. Sometimes men ask, How is it that the subject is so rarely touched in sermons? Mainly, I think, for a good reason. A preacher's business is to deal with principles, rather than particular details: as to which last right-minded men and women can judge for themselves, if they are willing to use their judgment. External pressure has often been found worse than useless in matters of fashion. Spirits which are otherwise meek and docile, rise up in angry rebellion against interference with their liberty in these things. The will of the most arbitrary sovereigns, such as Henry VIII. of England and Paul of Russia, has been exerted in vain to control extravagance in dress. As often as they issued edicts against one fashion, their edicts were evaded by new devices as luxurious and fantastic as the old. Once or twice the moral influence of a great religious teacher has brought about a reform of manners which no power of despotism could accomplish. But such reforms have depended for their vitality on the free consent of their followers.

What has been ever the most effectual means of restraining worldliness in every form, is the influence of Christian men and women living in the world, who work like leaven through the mass insensibly. The example of seven thousand who have not bowed down the knee to Baal, silent though it be, has an influence more lasting than the prophecies and miracles of an Elijah. It is the bounden duty of all the faithful to take their place in this number: to carry out into the lesser, as well as the greater affairs of human life, the spirit of loyalty to Christ. This need not be done ostentatiously, but it should be done firmly; not of necessity by open protest, but at all events by passive resistance to bad fashions.

Each of you, my brothers and sisters, has a certain measure of power within your immediate circle: small perhaps when considered alone, but forming part of that great voice of the world which overawes us when it is collected together. We are daily using this power for good or evil. The momentous question for us is, Are we using for good or for evil the influence which we have with those who look up to us?

Fashions are like the winds. They come from a source which is out of sight, prevail with more or less violence, and then pass away, to be succeeded by an altered current, we know not how or why. The wind, whatever its origin, is tempered in its progress by every hill, by every tall building, and every tree; and the choice rests with us whether we will give it free admission; as when we open doors and windows to the genial air, or close them to exclude the storm. So, in regard to the world's fashions, it is possible for those who have an advantageous position to temper and modify them; and it is possible for everyone to do something towards accepting or resisting them. Our conduct in this respect is a significant measure of the degree in which we fulfil the Baptismal vow of renouncing the vain pomp and glory of the world.

Those who are highly favoured by nature have special opportunities, and also special temptations. Whether they will or no, they stand as an example to others. At the same time they are led to think too much of themselves. Admiration kindles self-esteem; and self-esteem craves more admiration to feed it. The love of praise grows the more for being indulged; and each change of fashion brings a new triumph to those who are beautiful. On the other hand, they who fall short in personal gifts are tempted to make up for their shortcomings artificially. Feeling the need of adornment, they hope to compensate for the inequalities of nature by being what is called fashionable. These are temptations on either side, and the main thing is to observe that they are so. Being recognized as a tempter's work, as such they may be resisted. In spiritual as in other warfare, it is important to see our enemy. As a general rule, the extreme of the world's fashion is led and followed by those who are called in Scripture "the children of this world," who have no ideas beyond this world. It is to be expected that they whom Christ calls "the children of light" should have a self-restraint and soberness of outward bearing, to correspond with their inner life. An intuitive sense of propriety, a sense of what is comely and harmonious, guides those who wish for guidance to suitable models for imitation. Even dress has a kind of dumb language of its own which expresses character, not indeed what we are, but what we wish the world to think us. As among men various professions affect certain styles of dress, so among women there is a visible distinction between those who wish to be respected and those who only care to be admired.

To pursue this question further is beyond my purpose. What I desire is to awaken the minds of any who have never seriously considered it. The world's ever-changing fashion in dress, in manners, and in other respects, presents an important study for those who live in the world, often touching the depths of religious principle. Blindly to follow the multitude is base and weak; yet there is more pride than genuine virtue in the wilful singularity which sets the world at naught. What is needful in this, as in other questions of duty, is an active, discerning spirit, alive to all that is excellent, pure at heart and sound in judgment, faithful in that which is least.

Let us not think of religion as too high and solemn to be concerned with the trifles of common life. Not so has the word of God been expounded by the Apostles of Christ. "Whatsoever ye do, do all to the glory of God." Our life is so much made up of trifles, that if the principles of Christian duty were banished from these, very little would remain. When we are bidden to present ourselves a living sacrifice to God through Christ, in reasonable service, it means that our daily conversation and behaviour should be hallowed by a sense of duty to Him. It is not in speaking of religious truths, and using sacred names, but in a love of goodness in all its practical forms, that a godly spirit shows itself. Religious language may become a mere idle custom, as in some families endearing language becomes an empty custom, so that brothers and sisters use words of tender affection when they least mean them. Thus it is possible for us to talk of the mercies of the Lord Jesus, and the graces of His Spirit, without feeling either. Where the living power of the Spirit is, it is not expressed in words alone, but flows like the blood from the heart through every vein.

The least things are not too insignificant to be brought within the range of religious influences. Accordingly, when St. Paul exhorts the Corinthian women to veil themselves, he gives as a reason "because of the angels." That is, as the words are understood by the best interpreters, he would have them think of the pure and holy spirits in whose presence they are, and therefore behave modestly in the congregation. I do not know that our life could be guided in such matters by a better rule than this: to speak and act as in the presence of angels. The thought of their invisible fellowship will often recall us to our better selves, when the fashion of the world is drawing us astray. If it should befall you, as may easily happen, to be in society where the voice of conscience is laughed down, and where the simplicity of modest innocence is despised, pray God that your eyes may be opened, like those of Elisha's servant, to see yourselves encompassed with an angelic host, as we read in 2 Kings vi. We have indeed much cause to apply to our day the spiritual lessons of the history of Israel in the days of the prophets. That mortal conflict between the worshippers of Baal and the worshippers of Jehovah, which came to a crisis between Jezebel and Elijah, is, as I said before, revived in our day; for it is in substance a conflict beween the spirit of self-indulgence and the spirit of holy self-control.

Let us not be deceived by the material prosperity of our time, which enables not only the rich, but some who might be called comparatively poor, to rival the "bravery of tinkling ornaments," of which Isaiah speaks in the terrible third chapter of his prophecy. Israel was prosperous under Ahab and Jezebel, until the famine came. According to God's mysterious order of government, the whole nation was visited for their national sins, because they had forsaken Him, and given their hearts to the prince of this world. The children asked bread, and there was none to give to them. Our present prosperity will not save us from similar judgment, if we forget the Lord our Saviour.

XXV. JOSIAH.

"Notwithstanding the Lord turned not from the fierceness of his great wrath, wherewith his anger was kindled against Judah, because of all the provocations that Manasseh had provoked him withal."—2 *Kings* xxiii. 26.

(*Fifteenth Sunday after Trinity*, P.M.)

THIS mournful sentence prepares us for the tragical conclusion of Josiah's reign. Of Josiah we are told that there was no king like him before or after, that "turned to the Lord, with all his heart, and with all his soul, and with all his might." The sacred historian had, nevertheless, to record how, after his death, four unhappy kings, his children, were deposed in rapid succession; how the Holy City which he had purified from idolatry was plundered and burned; how the entire Jewish people was led into captivity.

Most readers will observe the contrast which is implied in the text by the word "notwithstanding," between the good deeds of Josiah and the miseries which followed afterwards, beginning with his own untimely death. The Bible itself appears to suggest the question, "Why was God's anger so fierce against His people?" and to suggest also the answer, that Josiah's zeal was weighed against the provocations of Manasseh, and was found wanting.

I believe that the Holy Spirit sets before us here a very instructive lesson, one which is the more worthy of study, inasmuch as a large part of the prophetic books belong to this very period. The events of Josiah's reign throw light on the prophecies of Jeremiah, Ezekiel, Daniel, Habakkuk, and Zephaniah; for they were all contemporaries of King Josiah, sharing in the hopes which his reign inspired, and which were so bitterly disappointed.

From a child Josiah was zealous for the worship of the true God, and at the age of twenty, if not before, he began to demolish the idolatrous altars and emblems, and the carved or molten images, which had overspread the kingdom during Manasseh's long reign of more than half a century. It was a work which could not be effected all at once. Some time after Josiah's first attempts at reformation, Jeremiah prophesied against the enormous wickedness of the nation, and the multitude of their idols. "According to the number of thy cities are thy gods, O Judah."

Six years later, Josiah entered anew upon his task as a restorer of pure religion. He undertook the repair of the Temple, which was fallen into decay. Carpenters, builders, and masons were sent for; and musicians were instructed to prepare for a solemn service at the reopening of the Lord's house. While the work was in progress Hilkiah, the high priest, made a discovery which gives us a startling idea of the state of neglect into which the religion of Israel had fallen. He found the book of the Law of Moses in the Temple, where it had lain disregarded and unread, as in the present century some of the most valuable manuscripts of the Scriptures have been found amid lumber in Eastern monasteries. But there was this important difference. The book of the Law which Hilkiah found was for all intents and purposes a new book, even to him. Its contents were unfamiliar to the men of that generation; and when it was read before the king and his council he became aware, for the first time, how grievously the law had been transgressed, and he rent his clothes for sorrow. Many needless doubts and speculations have been raised in connection with the discovery of this book. We have a parallel in modern history, when the eyes of the Reformers were opened to the contents of St. Paul's Epistles.[1]

There was a prophetess living in Jerusalem, Huldah by name; and to her Josiah sent to inquire further of the dreadful curses which are written in the book of Deuteronomy. She answered that wrath should be poured out upon Jerusalem, as it was written; but Josiah himself should die first, and not see it, because his heart was tender, and he had humbled himself. Thereupon the king acted as became him, with royal greatness of mind. He took the words of the prophetess as a warning to serve God more diligently, not as a decree of fate to be borne with folded hands. He sent and gathered the elders of Judah and Jerusalem, the priests, the prophets, and all the people. He read the book of the Law publicly before them, and solemnly vowed obedience. The whole assembly likewise pledged themselves, as of old at Mount Sinai, to the covenant of God. From such a beginning the best hopes might have

---

[1] See Green's "Short History of England," p. 299.

been formed. God has often shown that His judgments may be averted by repentance. We see an example in the Ninevites, who repented at the preaching of Jonah, and were spared. According to Ezekiel (chapter xxxiii.), a door of pardon is still open, though God has said, "Thou shalt surely die." And in the xxxvith chapter of Jeremiah we read how, after this renewed covenant of Josiah, the prophet was bidden to invite Judah to return from their evil ways, holding out a hope of forgiveness. At all events, God is God, to be obeyed to the death, happen what may.

After making this public covenant with God, Josiah persevered in his course of reformation with more energy than ever. The law of Moses was put severely in force. Vessels which had been used for the worship of Baal and the stars, both in the Lord's house and elsewhere, were taken outside the city as polluted things, and cast into a fire. Images and furniture of all kinds, used to adorn the foul orgies of idolaters, were similarly destroyed. The valley of Hinnom, in which children were made to pass through the fire to Moloch, was marked with such enduring desecration that its name Gehenna became a synonym for hell. One after another of the scandalous monuments of heathendom, the chariot and horses of the Sun, the altars of Ahaz, the altars of Manasseh, the more ancient altars of the gods of Sidon and Moab and Ammon, which Solomon had introduced in his dotage, all were defiled, the images broken and crushed to powder, the groves cut down, and the sites strewn with human bones.

Then the king went over into Samaria, and destroyed the famous altar which Jeroboam had erected at Bethel. The second book of the Kings and the second book of the Chronicles give copious particulars of the destruction, which Josiah superintended both in Judah and in Israel. No pity for the living, nor respect for the dead, was allowed to check the sweeping work of reformation. Only one grave was honoured, that of the man of God who had foretold these things, when Jeroboam first set up his golden calves. Josiah gave commandment, " Let no man move his bones."

And now, having returned to Jerusalem, he celebrated a passover such as had never been held before, at least within the memory of living men. So ended the eighteenth year of his reign, the twenty-sixth of his age.

But superstition is tenacious of life, and dies

hard. Although Josiah had changed the face of his kingdom, there still remained many secret abominations in the land. It was full of sorcerers, wizards, and dealers in magic. Such persons are always found where a right faith is wanting. Men cannot ignore the unseen powers about them, and those who reject the Spirit of the true God must needs invent false spirits, if only to satisfy an instinctive craving of the mind. If the finger of God is not discerned in the wonders of Nature, those wonders are ascribed by foolish men to lower spiritual agencies, and artful men profess a skill in sorcery as a means of imposing upon the weak. To get rid of these deceivers was Josiah's next undertaking. He suppressed the dealers in magic wherever he could find them, together with all remaining traces of the old idolatry and heathen corruption. In all these things Josiah did well: what more remained for him to do? He had restored the public worship of the Lord Jehovah with extraordinary splendour. He had restored the Divine Law of the Old Covenant. He had swept away the mass of abominations which provoked God's anger. He had turned to the Lord with all his heart and soul and strength. No form of evil had escaped his vigilance or resisted his energy. What, then, remained for him to do?

It remained for him to be quiet, to watch patiently over the new order which he had established. No longer with brilliant display of activity, but with sober, careful perseverance, he had to guard the growth of the institutions which he had planted afresh in Judah. The old rank weeds of heathenism had been cleared from the surface, but the root was scarcely touched. Years must elapse, and a new generation must arise, before the establishment of true religion could be completed. Above all things it should have been Josiah's study to train up his successor in the fear of God, placing his children under the care of wise and good men, and watching over their education. What he had done so far had only, in the words of the prophet, healed the hurt of his people slightly. The religion of Judah, like a broken limb new set, required time to grow strong again.

Under this trial Josiah's patience failed. He turned aside impetuously to a new enterprise. Pharaoh Necho, the King of Egypt, went up with an army past the northern frontier of Judah to encounter the King of Assyria, and Josiah advanced to intercept him. He was warned in vain that Pharaoh had no quarrel with him. The ambassadors of Pharaoh brought a message from their master, saying, "What have I to do with thee, thou King of Judah? I come not against thee. . . . . Forbear thee from meddling with God, who is with me, that He destroy thee not."

According to the apocryphal book of Esdras (I. i. 28) Jeremiah warned him to the same effect, but the king would heed no remonstrance, and advanced to battle.

The two hosts, of Judah and Egypt, met on the plain of Megiddo, "the place which is called in the Hebrew tongue Armageddon,"[1] for the battlefield of kings in the Apocalypse is named after the scene of Josiah's great defeat. He was mortally wounded by the Egyptian archers; and his servants brought his dead body in his chariot to Jerusalem. There the whole people lamented him with inconsolable grief. Jeremiah expressed the feeling of his countrymen when he cried, "The breath of our nostrils, the anointed of the Lord, was taken in their pits, of whom we said, Under his shadow we shall live among the heathen."[2]

---

[1] Revelation xvi. 16.   [2] Lamentations iv. 20.

Josiah's death was the ruin of his work in Judah. His sons turned back to the old corruptions of idolatry. Of one after another it is written, "he did evil in the sight of the Lord." Moreover, the foreign war, which he had presumptuously brought upon his kingdom, was its destruction. Pharaoh deposed his heir, and carried him into exile. Another son, placed on the throne by the King of Egypt, had the King of Assyria for his enemy. Only twelve years elapsed before the third son of Josiah was driven from the throne to a prison at Babylon, with his eyes put out; and the last remnants of the Jewish nation were carried away with him.

Statesmen and rulers are especially concerned in the lesson of this history, that the removal of abuses is only a superficial benefit, that morbid energy undoes its own good work, that time and patience are indispensable to a lasting reformation. But we may also find in the experience of private life an application of Josiah's example. For we have in his career a parallel to that which takes place in many an earnest and zealous mind. When we first enter upon the government of ourselves, that is, when we become conscious of moral responsibility, we perceive idols in the high places of our hearts, which need to be cast away; and close self-examination discovers a multitude of passions, humours, fancies, habits, which need to be reformed. Like Josiah, we may have made in our youth some efforts at amendment, but it is only in manhood that we can understand the sinfulness of our nature. Then, also, our eyes are opened to the contents of God's Word more clearly than ever before. Our High Priest, the Lord Jesus Christ Himself, makes known to us the message of the Gospel, and superintends the repair of God's Temple within us, the Temple of our body and spirit. We vow afresh to keep His Covenant in the solemn rite of Confirmation, and in the Sacrament of Holy Communion we celebrate the Passover of the Kingdom of Heaven. In these particulars the spiritual life of many a Christian soul resembles the career of Josiah; and so far, he is a noble example of holiness. It is with good reason that he is so often held up to the young as a model for imitation. His fervent love of God, his manly trust, his humble submissiveness and tender conscience, are lights to the world. Yet they who most resemble him in fervour of spirit have most cause to take warning by his presumption. If the spirit of Christ has wrought a great reform in you, do not hastily suppose that the reform is complete, and that you can proceed victoriously to other enterprises. The enemies of your soul, the world, the flesh, and the devil, are beaten down, not killed; and your lifelong task will be to form a habit of dominion over them. In the assiduous discharge of common duties, in the repression of evil thoughts and desires by a steady continuance in well-doing, your virtue will be exercised and built up by the grace of the Holy Spirit. But if you are ambitious to be always doing great things, if, after the excitement of reformation or conversion has done its work, you long for more excitement, you will be in danger of frustrating God's grace. The presumptuous spirit of new converts is too apt to meddle in matters which are too high for them. Freshly emerged from darkness into light, they aspire to do battle with the most formidable adversaries, to cast down the strongholds of Rome, or to challenge modern Science on its progressive march. In such cases the enemy may say, as we read in the Chronicles that Pharaoh said, "Forbear thee from meddling," and a rash encounter may bring defeat, not only on the eager champion, but on the cause which he represents. Good intentions are not enough to accomplish God's will. Even in His service there are limits to our several duties, which He teaches us by many signs; and it is a trial of faith to keep within those limits. "In quietness and in confidence shall be your strength." Saving faith is not faith in ourselves, or in our own special mission, but faith in God Who orders all things well, with us or without us: Who depends on none of His ministers, but ordains to each their bounds, saying, "Thus far shalt thou go, and no farther." Under all conditions of life our salvation stands in the grace of God through Jesus Christ. Our part is to do His will meekly in the place which He has assigned to us: having received His word in an honest and good heart, to keep it, and to bring forth fruit with patience.

XXVI. ESTHER.

"Who knoweth whether thou art not come to the kingdom for such a time as this?"—*Esther* iv. 14.

THE book of Esther, in common with the rest of Holy Scripture, has a close application to human life in every age. Although it has not the wealth of spiritual instruction which we find in some parts of the prophetic writings, it is pervaded by a spirit of religious and patriotic self-devotion. When Mordecai endeavoured to rouse his cousin, Queen Esther, to take the part of the oppressed Jews, he told her that, if she held her peace and refused her aid, some other way of deliverance would be found for the chosen people, but she and her father's house would be destroyed. That is, the guilt would lie on her head for not making a good use of her opportunity. Esther, with heroic courage, resolved to risk her life, by making intercession for her people. She sought for strength in united prayer and fasting for three days.

"Go," she said, "gather together all the Jews in Shushan and fast ye for me : .... I also and my maidens will fast likewise, and so will I go in unto the king, which is not according to the law; and if I perish, I perish."

Some have objected to this book, that it does not mention God's name. Yet it has been admitted and retained among the Canonical books of Holy Scripture, and I think the objection may be easily answered. The name of God is suppressed, out of reverence for His unspeakable Majesty. Faith in His protecting care of His people is manifest in the words of Mordecai, and throughout the whole book. Esther's request to her fellow-countrymen to fast for her, plainly implies a wish for their prayers. An under-current of religion, deep and strong, and not the less fervent for being restrained in utterance, pervades the book of Esther. The sacred writer seems to have acted according to the words of the Psalmist, "I will keep my mouth as it were with a bridle, while the ungodly is in my sight." In certain conditions of society men of deep spiritual feeling shrink from a free use of religious language. We have in our day examples of men who, like the author of the "Christian Year," are so sensitive in their religious awe of God, that they hide more than they express of their devotion.[1] The captivity of the Jews in Persia among the worshippers of idol gods had an influence of this kind upon them, as when the exiles by the waters of Babylon would not sing the Lord's song in a strange land.

The main subject of the book of Esther is the duty of patriotism, a duty sacred in the eyes of all nations, but peculiarly sacred to the Jews, because of their special calling as a nation. This book is a history of the origin of the feast of "Purim," or lots; showing how the Divine Providence, which watched our Israel, overruled the lots which Haman cast, so that the day which he thought to be propitious for their destruction, became a day of victory to them. Esther's favour with the king, and her devoted love for her nation, served as the means of this great deliverance. Thus the book is on one hand a memorial of God's mercy, and on the other hand of the Jewish Queen's patriotism. A similar combination of religious and national sentiment is common throughout Holy Scripture. It animates the song of triumph which Miriam

[1] See "Christian Year." Third Sunday after Epiphany.

sang by the Red Sea, the song of Deborah, and many of the Psalms. It is to be found in the Epistles of St. Paul, exalted, but not diminished by the spiritual enlightenment of the New Covenant. He writes to the Romans, "Brethren, my heart's desire and prayer for Israel is, that they might be saved." .... "I could wish that myself were accursed from Christ for my brethren, my kinsmen according to the flesh."

Sentences like these are sometimes quoted, to exhort us to sympathy with the Jewish nation. We owe so much to the Jews as guardians of God's revealed word, that the Apostle has a fair claim to our sympathy. But the more genuine application of his words is to our own people. What he felt for his fellow-countrymen we should feel for ours. We are not Jews, but Englishmen. In the good providence of God we have been born into a citizenship which draws us together by sacred bonds of duty and affection. The national spirit of the Bible should teach us a similar spirit of loyalty to our fellow-countrymen, while it is a stepping-stone to the larger charity of the citizens of Christ's universal kingdom.

Nationality has two aspects, one noble, the other base. Its baser aspect was seen among the Jews in our Lord's time, when it assumed the form of hatred against the Gentiles; when they persecuted St. Paul from city to city; and when, at the mere mention of his mission to the Gentiles, they cried, "Away with such a fellow from the earth, for it is not fit that he should live." Parallel cases may too easily be found in modern times, when nationality has been set against a large humanity; when the laws of justice and mercy have been ignored in dealing with foreign nations, and the pretext of national interest or glory has been held to justify public crimes. This is the baser aspect of nationality. Its nobler aspect is shown in contrast to the selfish love of ease and pleasure and private advantage; and this aspect is illustrated by many heroic deeds, of which Queen Esther's is one.

She had been raised from the condition of a captive to that of a Queen. Her life was made delightful by every resource of Persian luxury, but all the magnificence which surrounded her hung on the favour of a hasty-tempered king, one word from whom might dismiss her to death or degradation. Death was the penalty of intruding into his presence-chamber unbidden, unless he extended his sceptre in token of mercy.

Nevertheless, she would not shrink from putting her life in jeopardy, for love of her people. She pleaded for them before the king, first asking them to remember her in their prayers.

We stand at the present day in great need of this noble form of nationality. Of the baser kind there is enough, and more than enough. Wherever English travellers wander, or English vessels touch, they are apt to leave behind a reputation of national arrogance. But the better kind of national spirit, that which consists in self-sacrifice for the public good, is comparatively wanting. The same man who glories abroad in being an Englishman, is found at home compromising the interest and honour of his country for private advantage. There is a growing tendency to selfishness in conduct, and even in avowed principle. The first murderer's question, "Am I my brother's keeper?" is asked as a serious ethical inquiry. Unselfish patriotism or public spirit is so rare, that it is apt to be regarded more as a chivalrous extravagance than as the plain duty of every man and woman. And yet there is in the depths of our conscience a sense of the beauty and nobleness of self-sacrifice. The Spirit of God pleads against our selfish instincts on behalf of the Church and nation of which we are members, and on behalf of all mankind so far as our means of influence extend. The example of Esther's patriotism must needs move every one, whose mind is not so warped by selfish interest as to be unable to appreciate generous actions.

It is an example which especially concerns those who, like Esther, have the personal charm of beauty or fascination which wins the hearts of others. They have an immense power for good, if they will use it so. Often, unhappily, these gifts are wasted in selfish greed of admiration. An idle round of what is hardly to be called pleasure consumes time and talents, which might relieve not a little of the miseries of the poor. Extravagant and frivolous, if not vicious pastimes, bring many a woman, who might have been a heroine, to premature weariness of life,

> "In glowing health, with boundless wealth,
> But sickening of a vague disease,"

that lassitude which comes from a surfeit of self-indulgence, for which the English language has no name, without borrowing from the French. A self-indulgent soul is blighted by the operation of certain laws of nature. If, after the manner of most Eastern Queens, Esther had lived for herself alone, she would have tasted the bitterness of the cup of earthly pleasure. She would have found how vain is the splendour of a royal court, gold and jewels, costly apparel, chambers of carved and fragrant wood, halls of variegated marble, obedient slaves, gardens, fountains, instruments of music, luscious fruits, all that can please the eye, the ear, the taste. The sympathy for her oppressed people, which love dictated, was also true wisdom, and made her in the end a happier woman. There can be no spiritual peace with God in a life, which is given up to seeking pleasure and shrinking from pain.

Some there are, doubtless, who can go through such a life without compunction. Probably there are not a few who, in Esther's position, would have shut their ears to the appeal of Mordecai, and hardened their hearts against their kindred. Such callous natures are not to be envied. It is told in an ancient fable how a crew of intemperate mariners were transformed into beasts, and the degradation which they underwent, is rightly deemed to be increased by their satisfaction in being as they are:

> "They, so perfect is their misery,
> Not once perceive their foul disfigurement,
> But boast themselves more comely than before."

To be degraded, and to like it, is the most abject degradation. For as long as there is a spark of life in the conscience, there is hope of recovery by the grace of God. Painful as it is, the pang of self-reproach is blessed, like the throbs and thrills of the blood in those who are saved from drowning, which prove that life is not extinct. But for those who are base, and have no sense of dishonour in their baseness, hope is shut out. Divine life is quenched within them, and they have become as the beasts that perish.

Our generation has a wide field for that sympathy which, more than any other emotion, uplifts human nature from utter baseness. If we seek a parallel for the self-sacrifice of Esther, opportunities are not hard to find. There is a great work for charitable women in the present day, to bridge over the wide interval which separates class and class. Instead of a captive people among aliens, like the Jews in Persia, we have to do with the mass of our brethren, of whom multitudes are crushed under the iron wheels of a selfish civilization. If you know not whom to help, try the nearest at hand. Possibly there may be some one under your own roof, or very close to you, who needs the word of kindly sympathy which you can give, and which would bless you in the act of giving.

Consider the two motives by which Mordecai appeals to Esther, for both have a practical application. It is your privilege to be useful, and it is also your duty. God can fulfil His purpose by other means. He is able to dispense with our service, as Mordecai told Esther that God could dispense with hers, and bring enlargement to his people otherwise. Thus it is a high privilege to be the instrument of His benevolent purposes. But it is not the less a duty. "Who knoweth whether thou art not come to the kingdom for such a time as this?"

I might pursue this subject further into many details of common life, but the example of the patriotic and compassionate Queen of Persia leads our thoughts, by an obvious connection, to the great national event which is being celebrated at this time throughout the British Empire, the completion of fifty years of the reign of our beloved Queen. In this fact, apart from personal considerations, we have cause to thank God. An unbroken continuity of peaceful and orderly government is in itself a blessing. No hostile foot has trodden our English ground. No civil war has armed our citizens against each other, as in Paris, Berlin, and Vienna. During the past half century, the social prosperity of the nation has wonderfully increased. The population has nearly doubled, Colonies have been planted in every quarter of the globe. Great cities, rivalling the capitals of Italy and Spain, have sprung up in desert places of the southern hemisphere, peopled by Englishmen. Life has been made so much more easy and healthy, that its average duration has increased several years. Arts and Sciences have made unprecedented progress. National education, especially female education, has advanced enormously. The Church has undergone a revival which is felt wherever the English language is spoken. Our civil Constitution has been reformed without violent change, and the people are more free and more loyal than fifty years ago. Never was a reign so eventful, and yet so free from disastrous events. For all this we should render humble and hearty thanks to the King of kings.

But our thoughts must needs turn also with natural affection and loyalty to the person of her, who for these fifty years has been a mother to her people. On human virtues it is unfitting to enlarge in this place. I will venture, however, to say that we are the envy of other nations because of the pure, noble, and law-abiding character of our Sovereign. Those who are present at the solemn Thanksgiving Service in the Abbey of Westminster, next Tuesday,[1] will have much to move them in the spectacle; and many deep thoughts are suggested by the occasion; but none more tender than this, that the Queen of this great empire has been, like Esther, constant in love for her people and her people's God, unspoilt by the temptations of royalty, and always full of compassion for the afflicted.

While she kneels humbly before the throne of Him who is her King and ours, may the sceptre of His mercy be held out to her, and His ears be open to her supplication!

[1] June 21, 1887.

CHISWICK PRESS:—C. WHITTINGHAM AND CO., TOOKS COURT, CHANCERY LANE.

www.ingramcontent.com/pod-product-compliance
Lightning Source LLC
Chambersburg PA
CBHW030757230426
43667CB00007B/997